Series / Number 07-044

D0168715

CLUSTER ANALYSIS

MARK S. ALDENDERFER
Northwestern University

ROGER K. BLASHFIELD
University of Florida, Gainesville

SAGE PUBLICATIONS
The International Professional Publishers
Newbury Park   London   New Delhi

For information address:

SAGE Publications, Inc.
2111 West Hillcrest Drive
Newbury Park, California 91320

SAGE Publications Ltd.
28 Banner Street
London EC1Y 8QE
England

SAGE Publications India Pvt. Ltd.
M-32 Market
Greater Kailash I
New Delhi 110 048 India

International Standard Book Number 0-8039-2376-7

Library of Congress Catalog Card No. 84-051918

SEVENTH PRINTING, 1990

When citing a professional paper, please use the proper form. Remember to cite the
correct Sage University Paper series title and include the paper number. One of the
following formats can be adapted (depending on the style manual used):

(1) IVERSEN, GUDMUND R. and NORPOTH, HELMUT (1976) "Analysis of
Variance." Sage University Paper series on Quantitative Applications in the Social
Sciences, 07-001. Beverly Hills and London: Sage Pubns.

OR

(2) Iversen, Gudmund R. and Norpoth, Helmut. 1976. *Analysis of Variance.* Sage
University Paper series on Quantitative Applications in the Social Sciences, series no.
07-001. Beverly Hills and London: Sage Pubns.

CONTENTS

Series Editor's Introduction

Classification of objects into meaningful sets—clustering—is an important procedure in all of the social sciences. Yet, despite the widespread use of clustering notions, cluster analysis as a formal, multivariate statistical procedure is poorly understood. In part this is because techniques for clustering have developed very rapidly in the last 10 years, spurred most recently by the availability of computers to carry out the frequently awesome calculations involved. Their development and use by anthropologists, psychologists, political scientists, and sociologists, not to mention biologists, has also meant that terminology is often unstandardized and confusing and that new developments spread slowly through all of the relevant disciplines.

Cluster Analysis, by Mark Aldenderfer and Roger Blashfield, is designed to be an introduction to this topic for those with no background and for those who need an up-to-date and systematic guide through the maze of concepts, techniques, and algorithms associated with the clustering idea. The authors begin by discussing measures of similarity—the input needed to perform any clustering analysis. They note varying theoretical meanings of the concept and discuss the set of empirical measures most commonly used to measure similarity. Various methods for actually identifying the clusters are then described. Finally, the authors discuss procedures for validating the adequacy of a cluster analysis, a topic often neglected. At all points, the differing concepts and techniques are compared and evaluated.

Since cluster analysis of large data sets almost has to be done with the aid of a computer, the authors discuss a variety of standard and special purpose programs. In addition, a guide through additional literature is provided in each chapter. Raw data for the examples is included in the appendix so that readers can check their understanding of the procedures described as they work their way through them.

Because it pulls together literature from such a wide variety of sources, provides the reader with a thorough guide to current uses, statistical techniques, and computer programs, and is clearly organized and written, *Cluster Analysis* provides an invaluable addition to our series.

—Richard G. Niemi
Series Co-Editor

CLUSTER ANALYSIS

MARK S. ALDENDERFER
Northwestern University

ROGER K. BLASHFIELD
University of Florida, Gainesville

1. INTRODUCTION

An Ancient Chinese Classification of Animals
Animals are divided into (a) those that belong to the Emperor, (b) embalmed ones, (c) those that are trained, (d) suckling pigs, (e) mermaids, (f) fabulous ones, (g) stray dogs, (h) those that are included in this classification, (i) those that tremble as if they were mad, (j) innumerable ones, (k) those drawn with a very fine camel's hair brush, (l) others, (m) those that have just broken a flower vase, and (n) those that resemble flies from a distance (Jorge Luis Borges, *Other Inquisitions: 1937-1952*).

Classification is a basic human conceptual activity. Children learn very early in their lives to classify the objects in their environment and to associate the resulting classes with nouns in their language. Classification is also a fundamental process of the practice of science since classificatory systems contain the concepts necessary for the development of theories within a science.

"Cluster analysis" is the generic name for a wide variety of procedures that can be used to create a classification. These procedures empirically form "clusters" or groups of highly similar entities. More specifically, a clustering method is a multivariate statistical procedure that starts with a data set containing information about a sample of entities and attempts to reorganize these entities into relatively homogeneous groups.

Clustering methods have been recognized throughout this century, but most of the literature on cluster analysis has been written during the past two decades. The major stimulus for the development of clustering methods was a book entitled *Principles of Numerical Taxonomy*, published in 1963 by two biologists, Robert Sokal and Peter Sneath. Sokal and Sneath argued that an efficient procedure for the generation of biological classifications would be to gather all possible data on a set of

7

organisms of interest, estimate the degree of similarity among these organisms, and use a clustering method to place relatively similar organisms into the same groups. Once groups of similar organisms were found, the membership of each group could be analyzed to determine if they represented different biological species. In effect, Sokal and Sneath assumed that "pattern represented process"; that is, the patterns of observed differences and similarities among organisms could be used as a basis for understanding the evolutionary process.

The literature on cluster analysis exploded after the publication of the Sokal and Sneath book. The number of published applications of cluster analysis in all scientific fields has doubled approximately once every three years from 1963 to 1975 (Blashfield and Aldenderfer, 1978b). This rate of growth is much faster than that of even the most rapidly growing disciplines, such as biochemistry. There are two reasons for the rapid growth of the literature on cluster analysis: (1) the development of high-speed computers and (2) the fundamental importance of classification as a scientific procedure. Before computers, clustering methods were cumbersome and computationally difficult when applied to the large data sets in which most classifiers were interested. To cluster a data set with 200 entities requires searching a similarity matrix with 19,900 unique values. To search manually through a matrix of this size is a staggering and time-consuming task that few researchers (or their unlucky assistants) are willing to undertake. With the widespread availability of the computer, the time-consuming process of handling large matrices became feasible.

The second reason for the growth of interest in clustering is that all sciences are built upon classifications that structure their domains of inquiry. A classification contains the major concepts used in a science. The classification of elements, for instance, is the basis for understanding inorganic chemistry and the atomic theory of matter; the classification of diseases provides the structural basis for the science of medicine. Since clustering methods are viewed as objective, easily replicable ways to construct classifications, they have enjoyed widespread popularity across seemingly diverse scientific disciplines.

The social sciences have long maintained an interest in cluster analysis. Among the earliest of these studies were those by anthropologists who defined homogeneous culture areas by using methods of matrix manipulation (Czekanowski, 1911; see also Driver, 1965; Johnson, 1972). In psychology, cluster analysis was viewed as a "poor man's factor analysis" by one of its major proponents (Tryon, 1939). Other disciplines, most notably political science, were also involved in the early development of clustering in the social sciences. Although many of the theories and applications that served as the basis for clustering in the past have been repudiated by later generations of scholars, all social sciences now have strong modern traditions in the use of clustering methods.

Despite their popularity, clustering methods are still poorly understood in comparison to such multivariate statistical procedures as factor analysis, discriminant analysis, and multidimensional scaling. The social sciences literature on clustering reflects a bewildering and often contradictory array of terminology, methods, and preferred approaches. Published guidance for the novice is sparse, and this, combined with the diversity of terminology and methodology, has created a complex maze that is virtually impenetrable. The goal of this book is to guide the novice through the maze of cluster analysis. Because of the tremendous diversity of methods that have been proposed over the past twenty years, we do not exhaustively review all or even most of these methods. Instead, we emphasize those methods and procedures that are comparatively well known in the social sciences or that we believe have strong merit for use in applied research.

How Clustering Methods Are Used

As we have already noted, clustering methods are designed to create homogeneous groups of cases or entities called clusters. Most of the varied uses of cluster analysis can be subsumed under four principal goals:

(1) development of a typology or classification,
(2) investigation of useful conceptual schemes for grouping entities,
(3) hypothesis generation through data exploration, and
(4) hypothesis testing, or the attempt to determine if types defined through other procedures are in fact present in a data set.

Of these goals, the creation of classifications probably accounts for the most frequent use of clustering methods, but in most cases of applied data analysis, many of these goals are combined to form the basis of the study. To understand these goals better, consider the following illustrations of the use of cluster analysis.

Alcoholism is a major mental health problem in this country, but no classification of alcoholics has ever gained wide acceptance among mental health professionals. Goldstein and Linden (1969), two clinical psychologists, used cluster analysis to build a classification of alcoholics. They gathered data on 513 alcoholics who had been admitted to a rehabilitation program at a state hospital in Indianapolis, Indiana. The data gathered on these patients were from a commonly used psychological test, the Minnesota Multiphasic Personality Inventory (MMPI). This test contains 566 true/false items that are standardly summarized in terms of 13 scales that have diagnostic significance (e.g., the Schizophrenia scale and the Hysteria scale).

Goldstein and Linden subdivided their data into two parts: a derivation subsample (239 patients) and a replication subsample (251 patients). Using the derivation subsample, they formed a 239 × 239 correlation matrix that represented the similarities among the MMPI profiles from these patients, and used a clustering method devised by Lorr (1966). Of the patients in the derivation subsample, 114 were assigned to four clusters, while the remaining 125 patients were not assigned to any cluster. When the same steps were performed on the replication subsample, four clusters were again found that contained 106 (of the 251) alcoholics. The mean profiles of the clusters were basically the same across the two subsamples. The names that Goldstein and Linden assigned to these four clusters of alcoholics were (1) emotionally unstable personality, (2) psychoneurotic with anxiety/depression, (3) psychopathic personality, and (4) alcoholic with drug abuse and paranoid features.

The Goldstein and Linden study was important in the literature on alcoholism because it provided the model for more than 15 subsequent studies using cluster analysis to classify alcoholics. Most of these studies have provided general support for the validity of the first two clusters (types I and II).

The second study examined was performed by two anthropologists, Burton and Romney (1975). Their goal was to determine on what basis speakers of English classified role terms. The data used in the study were the results of a simple sorting of the 58 most common role terms in the language. Typical of the terms included in the study were "artist," "boss," "friend," "man," "owner," "poet," and "spy." Those who participated in the study were given each of these terms on a separate piece of paper and asked to look at the terms and then to place them into whatever groups came to mind. No limits were placed on the number or size of the groups. The similarity between the groups of role terms was computed using the Z measure, commonly used with sorting-task data (Miller, 1969).

The authors first investigated the similarity data with nonmetric multidimensional scaling in an attempt to determine if any underlying structure could be used to describe the patterns of similarity of the role terms. A three-dimensional solution was deemed valid. The dimensions were interpreted as an evaluative dimension in which terms such as "gambler," "gunman," and "spy" were contrasted with terms such as "friend" and "companion"; a power dimension in which formal roles such as "boss" or "foreman" were contrasted with kin terms and other intimate terms such as "friend"; and an occupational dimension that simply contrasted job roles with all other role terms. They then performed a hierarchical cluster analysis using two different methods on the similarity data. The authors chose the eight-cluster solution for each of the methods, and noted that the results from the two clustering methods, while different in many respects, nevertheless had four major clusters in common: (1) a cluster of seven kin terms, (2) a cluster of friends, (3) a cluster of social-category membership terms, and (4) a cluster of managerial roles. They concluded that the results obtained from the two multivariate methods were complementary, and suggested that those individuals who sorted the terms made their decisions both on the global criteria recovered by the multidimensional scaling (the dimensions of evaluation, power, and occupation) and the more finely tuned criteria suggested by the clustering of terms, such as the clear hierarchical structure of English kinship terms based upon degree of relationship between individuals regardless of sex. The results of the cluster analysis corroborated the ambiguity of sex roles in Western society that has been reported in other anthropological studies, and further clarified the basis upon which speakers of English classify kinship terms.

The final example, a sociological study by Filsinger, Faulkner, and Warland (1979), was designed to create a classification of religious individuals. The data were gathered using the Religiosity Scale (DeJong et al., 1976) which was administered in a questionnaire format to 547 undergraduate students at Pennsylvania State University. A total of 37 items were chosen from the Religiosity Scale, a measurement device based upon a previous factor analysis of these data (DeJong et al., 1976). Since the entire sample of 574 students was too large to analyze economically, a sample of 220 were selected for the study. A 220 × 220 similarity matrix between pairs of individuals was clustered. The authors chose the seven-cluster solution for interpretation, and named seven types of religious individuals:

Type I: outsiders
Type II: conservatives
Type III: rejectors
Type IV: moderately religious
Type V: marginally religious
Type VI: orthodox
Type VII: culturally religious

Filsinger et al. also attempted to validate their classification. First they performed a discriminant analysis on the clusters, and the results were said to be highly significant.[1] Second, they compared the subjects in the various clusters by using seven demographic variables. On four of the seven variables, (size of home community, political identification, percentage of students not associated with the church, and religious affiliation), the clusters were significantly different. The authors concluded that overall results provided support for their empirical typology of religious individuals.

Each of the goals of cluster analysis can be found in the examples. The building of classifications was the most important goal of the Goldstein and Linden, and Filsinger et al. studies, but the exploration of the classification schemes (the MMPI and the Religiosity Scale) figured prominently as well. The study by Burton and Romney was devoted primarily to data exploration and hypothesis testing, and the building of a formal classification was of secondary importance. In this case, while the hypothesis testing was not conducted formally, the authors observed that the results corroborated findings about the use of language that had been discovered through more traditional anthropological methods.

A consideration of the three examples also shows that despite differences in goals, data types, and methods used, five basic steps characterize all cluster analysis studies.

(1) selection of a sample to be clustered
(2) definition of a set of variables on which to measure the entities in the sample
(3) computation of the similarities among the entities
(4) use of a cluster analysis method to create groups of similar entities
(5) validation of the resulting cluster solution

Each of these steps is essential to the use of cluster analysis in applied data analysis, and each is discussed at length below.

Data Sets to Be Used as Examples

We will use one data set to illustrate how clustering methods are used, and one is presented in the Appendix. It is included so that interested readers can experiment with the procedures we illustrate; our results can be used as benchmarks for comparison.

The first example data set is a hypothetical collection of human burials and their accompanying artifacts from an archaeological site. Burial data are important to archaeologists because they may contain information about the social statuses or roles played by the individuals found in the graves. By carefully analyzing the contents of graves, archaeologists may be able to infer the status differences among individuals that in turn may lead to inferences about the nature of social ranking and level of development of the society that created them.

The data set varies across three dimensions: age, sex, and status. At our hypothetical archaeological site 25 individuals have been "interred," and they are divided into three age groups: children, adolescents, and adults. Two statuses are also present: elite and nonelite. Each grave may contain up to eight different artifactual types: local ceramics, arrow points, shell bead bracelets, chipped stone, bone pins, bone awls, imported ceramics, and metal. Each of these artifact types has a status and sex distribution; age distinctions in artifact types have not been included in the data so that the structure of the data set can remain relatively simple. The data are coded in binary form, with the simple presence or absence of the artifact recorded.

The second data set, also based upon artificial data, has been structured to represent the type of classification problem that is often addressed in psychopathology. The basic data set contains 90 hypothetical patients who represent three types of mental disorders: psychoses (P), neuroses (N), and character disorders (CD). Thirty patients were created to represent each of these general groups. Details of the data generation process can be found in Blashfield and Morey (1980). The variables used to assess the patients were the 13 standard scales from the MMPI, the psychological test described earlier in the Goldstein and Linden (1969) study of alcoholics. The names for these scales, with the abbreviations for each, are

● Validity Scales
  L—Lie scale
  F—"Fake bad" scale
  K—Correction scale

● Clinical Scales
  Hs—Hypochondriasis
  D—Depression
  Hy—Hysteria
  Pd—Psychopathic Deviate
  Mf—Male/Female scale
  Pa—Paranoia
  Pt—Psychasthenia
  Sc—Schizophrenia
  Ma—Hypomania
  Si—Social Introversion

Briefly, the MMPI consists of 566 true/false items that are all stated in the first person (e.g., "I like mechanics magazines."). The 566 items are organized into scales on the MMPI using an empirical keying approach. During its development, the MMPI was administered to both normal individuals and psychiatric patients. An item was assigned to a scale if it separated a clinical group from the normals, regardless of the content of the item. All ten "clinical" scales were created using this approach, and the names of the scales represent the diagnostic groups that these scales were intended to predict. The other three standard scales on the MMPI are validity scales that measure the degree to which a patient may be falsely exaggerating, denying, or otherwise modifying his or her symptoms.

MMPI results are interpreted by referring to patient profiles. Figure 1 shows the MMPI results for one of the 90 patients used in the example data set. Scores are plotted on the profile for each scale, with 50 representing the score of normals, and 70 indicating a significant deviation from normality. Profiles are distinguished primarily on the basis of "peaks," or the scales that have the highest scores. For this patient, the high scores ranked in order are Pa, Sc, F, Pt, Si, and Ma, and this profile is fairly typical of a patient who is diagnosed as having paranoid schizophrenia.

A Few Cautions about Cluster Analysis

Before proceeding with chapters that discuss the basic methodological steps of cluster analysis, a few precautionary generalizations about cluster analysis must be made.

(1) *Most cluster analysis methods are relatively simple procedures that in most cases, are not supported by an extensive body of statistical reasoning.* In other words, most cluster analysis methods are heuristics (simple "rules of thumb"). They are little more than plausible algorithms that can be used to create clusters of cases. This stands in sharp contrast to factor analysis, for instance, which is based upon an extensive body of statistical reasoning. Although many clustering algorithms have important mathematical properties that have been explored in some detail (see Jardin and Sibson, 1971), it is important to recognize the fundamental simplicity of these methods. In doing so, the user is far less likely to make the mistake of reifying the cluster solution.

(2) *Cluster analysis methods have evolved from many disciplines and are inbred with the biases of these disciplines.* This is important to note, because each discipline has its own biases and preferences as to the kinds of questions asked of the data, the types of data thought to be useful in building a classification, and the structure of classifications thought to

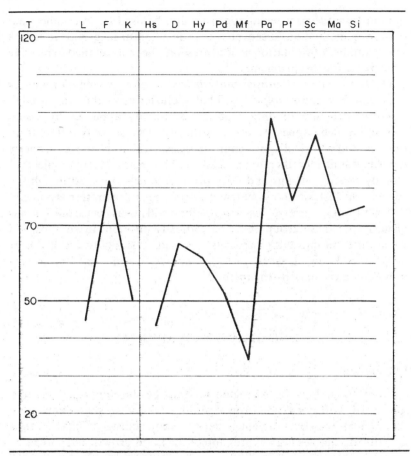

Figure 1: Example of MMPI Profile

be useful. What may be useful in psychology may not be useful to the biologist, and since clustering methods are often no more than plausible rules for creating groups, users must be aware of the biases that often accompany the presentation and description of a clustering method.

(3) *Different clustering methods can and do generate different solutions to the same data set.* The finding that different methods generate different solutions is common in most applied research. One reason for differences in solutions is that clustering methods have evolved from disparate sources that have emphasized different rules of group formation. While this may be a natural outgrowth of disciplinary specialization, it is nevertheless a source of considerable confusion for both novices and sophisticated users of cluster analysis. What is

obviously needed are techniques that can be used to determine what clustering method has discovered the most "natural" groups in a data set. A number of validation procedures have been developed to provide some relief for this problem.

(4) *The strategy of cluster analysis is structure-seeking although its operation is structure-imposing.* That is, clustering methods are used to discover structure in data that is not readily apparent by visual inspection or by appeal to other authority. This strategy differs from that embodied by discriminant analysis, which is more properly described as an identification procedure. This method assigns objects to already existing groups and does not create new ones. Although the strategy of clustering may be structure-seeking, its operation is one that is structure-imposing. A clustering method will always place objects into groups, and these groups may be radically different in composition when different clustering methods are used. The key to using cluster analysis is knowing when these groups are "real" and not merely imposed on the data by the method.

2. SIMILARITY MEASURES

Terminology

Many terms have been created to describe the important features concerned with the estimation of similarity. As we shall show later (Chapter 5), the development of jargon about cluster analysis within scientific disciplines is an expression of the rapid growth and spread of cluster analysis. Each discipline organizes its terminology in ways that may not necessarily overlap the terminology of other disciplines even if the terms are used to describe the same things. Unless the potential user of cluster analysis is aware of these terminological differences, considerable confusion can result.

The terms "case," "entity," "object," "pattern," and "OTU" (operational taxonomic unit) denote the "thing" being classified; whereas "variable," "attribute," "character," and "feature" denote those aspects of the "things" used to assess their similarity. Another set of important terms are "Q analysis" and "R analysis"; the former refers to the relationships between variables. Cluster analysis, for instance, has been traditionally described as a "Q-mode" technique, whereas factor analysis has been traditionally described as an "R-mode" method.

The potential user of cluster analysis should also note that data matrices are often organized in different ways. In the social sciences the convention is to describe the data set as a matrix consisting of N cases (the rows of the matrix) measured on P variables (the columns of the matrix). In the biological sciences this ordering is reversed, resulting in a P × N matrix of data. In this book, we reserve the term "raw data" to describe the original N × P matrix of cases and their variables before the calculation of similarity takes place. Accordingly, we will use the terms "similarity matrix" or "proximity matrix" to describe the N × N matrix of similarities of the cases after the raw data have been submitted to some measure of similarity.

Even the term "similarity" is not immune from varied meanings, and its synonyms are "resemblance," "proximity," and "association." However, other authors restrict the use of "similarity" to describe a limited set of coefficients. For instance, Everitt (1980) uses the term "similarity coefficient" to denote those measures which Sneath and Sokal (1973) call "association coefficients." Clifford and Stephenson (1975), to confuse things further, restrict the use of the term "association coefficient" to a meaning that is a subset of the definitions by either Everitt or Sneath and Sokal. We use the term "similarity coefficient" (or measure) to describe any type of similarity measure, and adhere to the classification of similarity coefficients proposed by Sneath and Sokal (1973), who subdivide these coefficients into four groups:

(1) correlation coefficients,

(2) distance measures,

(3) association coefficients, and

(4) probabilistic similarity measures.

Later in the chapter each of these groups will be briefly described.

The Concept of Similarity

That things are recognized as similar or dissimilar is fundamental to the process of classification. Despite its apparent simplicity, the concept of similarity, and especially the procedures used to measure similarity, are far from simple. Indeed, the concept of similarity raises basic epistemological problems such as, How can we form useful, abstract concepts to organize what we know? To answer that question, of course, one must be able to categorize things, and the process of categorization requires the lumping together of things that are perceived as similar. The problem of similarity, however, does not lie with the simple recognition that things are either alike or not alike, but instead in the ways in which these concepts are expressed and implemented in scientific research. To be successful, science must be based upon objective, replicable procedures; therefore, the development of statistical procedures to measure more "objectively" the similarity of things is a natural consequence of the necessity for replicable and reliable classifications.

The quantitative estimation of similarity has been dominated by the concept of *metrics*; this approach to similarity represents cases as points in a coordinate space such that the observed similarities and dissimilarities of the points correspond to metric distances between them (Tversky, 1977). The dimensionality of the space is determined by the number of variables used to describe the cases. There are four standard criteria that can be used to judge whether a similarity measure is a true metric. These are

(1) *Symmetry.* Given two entities, x and y, the distance, d, between them satisfies the expression

$$d(x,y) = d(y,x) \geq 0$$

(2) *Triangle inequality.* Given three entities, x, y, z, the distances between them satisfies the expression

$$d(x,y) \leq d(x,z) + d(y,z)$$

Obviously this simply states that the length of any side of a triangle is equal to or less than the sum of the other two sides. This concept has also been called the metric inequality.

(3) *Distinguishability of nonidenticals.* Given two entities x and y,

$$\text{if } d(x,y) \neq 0, \text{ then } x \neq y$$

(4) *Indistinguishability of identicals.* For two identical elements, x and x',

$$d(x,x') = 0$$

That is, the distance between the two entities is zero.

These are important mathematical properties, and many researchers, most notably Jardine and Sibson (1971) and Clifford and Stephenson (1975), have presented arguments against the routine use of similarity coefficients that do not meet the qualifications of a metric. Many, but not all, distance measures discussed below are metrics. A number of correlation measures are not metric. Coefficients that are not metrics may not be jointly monotonic; that is, the values of different coefficients used with the same data will not necessarily vary conjointly, raising the disturbing issue that these coefficients could suggest quite different relationships among the entities. The practical significance of determining whether a measure meets the criteria of being metric can be shown by noting that a popular similarity measure, the Pearson product-moment correlation coefficient, certainly fails to meet the third criterion, and as Clifford and Stephenson (1975) suggest, it may well not meet the second (i.e., the triangle inequality) in many applications.

Despite their obvious importance, metrics are by no means the only way to represent the similarity between objects. Certainly on philosophical grounds that are beginning to be supported by psychological research, it is possible to conceive of similarity as the comparison of features; thus the estimation of similarity can be based upon the process of feature matching (Tversky, 1977). This concept of similarity has no inherent dimensionality for the representation of resemblance. Moreover, there is a considerable body of social research in which the similarity between entities is directly estimated. This similarity, for example, may be based on the degree of relationship that exists between entities, and in this type of research, asymmetric similarity values are common. That is, entity A may stand in certain relation to B, but B may not have that degree of relation to A (e.g., Adam may be in love with Betty, but Betty may not like Adam at all). This type of relationship is also common in economics, where one nation can import more goods from another nation than it exports to that nation. Asymmetry presents special problems in the calculation of similarity coefficients. Tversky (1977) provides a good introduction to this issue.

The potential user of cluster analysis should be aware that many types of similarity exist, and that while many of the coefficients and measures commonly used in quantitative approaches to classification are metrics, there are alternatives to the use of these measures that may be appropriate and necessary within the context of research. The choice of similarity measure, then, should be embedded ultimately within the design of research, which is itself determined by the theoretical, practical, and philosophical context of the classification problem.

The Choice of Variables

Before describing popular coefficients used in the calculation of similarity, a brief digression needs to be made about the choice of variables and about data transformations prior to the calculation of similarity. The choice of variables to be used with cluster analysis is one of the most critical steps in the research process, but, unfortunately, it is one of the least understood as well. The basic problem is to find that set of variables that best represents the concept of similarity under which the study operates. Ideally, variables should be chosen within the context of an explicitly stated theory that is used to support the classification. The theory is the basis for the rational choice of the variables to be used in the study. In practice, however, the theory that supports classification research is often implicit, and in this situation it is difficult to assess the relevance of the variables to the problem.

The importance of using theory to guide the choice of variables should not be underestimated. The temptation to succumb to a naive empiricism in the use of cluster analysis is very strong, since the technique is ostensibly designed to produce "objective" groupings of entities. By "naive empiricism" we mean the collection and subsequent analysis of as many variables as possible in hope that the "structure" will emerge if only enough data are obtained. While empirical studies are important to the progress of any science, those that adopt an implicit naive empiricist perspective are dangerous in the context of cluster analysis because of the heuristic nature of the technique and the many unsolved problems that have plagued its application (Everitt, 1979).

In most statistical analyses the data are routinely standardized by some appropriate method. If the normality of a variable is in question, a logarithmic or other transformation is often performed. If the data are not of the same scale values, they are commonly standardized to a mean of 0 and to unit variance. There is some controversy, however, as to whether standardization should be a routine procedure in cluster analysis. As Everitt (1980) notes, standardization to unit variance and mean of 0 can reduce the differences between groups on those variables that may well be the best discriminators of group differences. It would be far more appropriate to standardize variables *within* groups (i.e., within clusters), but obviously this cannot be done until the cases have been placed into groups.

Edelbrock (1979) has noted that variables in multivariate data sets may have different distribution parameters across groups; thus standardization may not constitute an equivalent transformation of these variables and could possibly change the relationships between them. However, his Monte Carlo studies of the effects of standardization on subsequent analyses using the correlation coefficient and various hierarchical clustering methods did not reveal substantial differences between the use of standardized versus nonstandardized variables in the resulting classifications. Milligan (1980) has also found that standardization appears to have only a minor effect on the results of a cluster analysis. Others, most notably Matthews (1979), have shown that standardization did have a negative effect on the adequacy of the results of a cluster analysis when compared to an "optimal" classification of the cases under study.

The situation regarding standardization is far from clear. Users with substantially different units of measurement will undoubtedly want to standardize them, especially if a similarity measure such as Euclidean distance is to be used. The decision to standardize should be made on a problem-to-problem basis, and users should be aware that results may differ solely on the basis of this factor, although the magnitude of the effect will vary from data set to data set.

Other types of data transformation are possible, and many of these have been used concurrently with cluster analysis. Factor analysis or principal components analysis is often used when the researcher knows that the variables used in the study are highly correlated. The uncritical use of highly correlated variables to compute a measure of similarity is essentially an implicit weighting of these variables. That is, if three highly correlated variables are used, the effect is the same as using only one variable that has a weight three times greater than any other variable. Principal components analysis and factor analysis can be used to reduce the dimensionality of the data, thereby creating new, uncorrelated variables that can be used as raw data for the calculation of similarity between cases. Once again, there is controversy surrounding this procedure. Factor analysis tends to blur the relationship between clusters because it assumes that factor scores are normally distributed. The effect of factor analysis is to transform the data in such a way that any modes present are merged, resulting in variables that are normally distributed. Rohlf (1970) has noted that principal components analysis tends to maintain the representation of widely separated clusters in a reduced space but also minimizes—and thus blurs—the distances between clusters or groups that are not widely separated.

The problem of whether or not to weight variables has also aroused considerable controversy. Most of this debate has taken place within the biological sciences. Weighting is simply the manipulation of a value of a variable such that it plays a greater or lesser role in the measurement of similarity between two cases (Williams, 1971). While the concept of weighting is simple, its practice is difficult, and very few guidelines exist. Williams describes five types of weighting, the most common being the a priori manipulation of variables. Sneath and Sokal (1973) argue strongly against a priori weighting, and suggest that the appropriate way to measure similarity is to give all variables equal weight. This advice, however, must be tempered with the understanding that the Sneath and Sokal view of clustering is considered a radically empirical approach to the creation of classifications. In many instances it may well make sense to weight a particular variable a priori if there are good theoretical reasons for this and there are well-defined procedures under which weighting can occur. While the issue of weighting has not yet become an issue of debate in the social sciences, researchers using clustering methods should be aware of the controversy.

Similarity Measures

Now that the problems of variable selection and data transformation have been discussed, a presentation of popular similarity coefficients can be offered. As noted earlier, there are four types of similarity measures: (1) correlation coefficients, (2) distance measures, (3) association coefficients, and (4) probabilistic similarity coefficients. Each of these methods has advantages and disadvantages that must be considered before a decision is made to use one. Although all four types have been used extensively by numerical taxonomists and others in the biological sciences, only correlation and distance coefficients have had widespread use in the social sciences. Correspondingly, we devote more discussion to these two types of measures.

CORRELATION COEFFICIENTS

These coefficients, often called angular measures because of their geometric interpretation, are among the most frequently used measures of similarity in the social sciences. The most popular is the product-moment correlation coefficient suggested by Karl Pearson. Originally defined for use as a method to correlate variables, it has been used in quantitative classification to determine the correlation between cases. In this context, the coefficient is defined as

$$r_{jk} = \frac{\Sigma(x_{ij} - \bar{x}_j)(x_{ik} - \bar{x}_k)}{\sqrt{\Sigma(x_{ij} - \bar{x}_j)^2 (x_{ik} - \bar{x}_k)^2}}$$

where x_{ij} is the value of variable i for case j, $\bar{x}_j$ is the mean of all values of the variables for case j, and n is the number of variables. The method is used with ratio or interval scale variables, and in the case of binary data it is transformed into the familiar phi coefficient. The value of the coefficient ranges from -1 to $+1$, and a value of zero indicates no relationship between the cases. Since the mean of each case is summed across all variables of each case, standard significance tests of r have no obvious meaning.

The correlation coefficient is frequently described as a *shape* measurement, in that it is insensitive to differences in the magnitude of the variables used to compute the coefficient. As Williams (1971) notes, Pearson's r is sensitive to shape because of its implicit standardization of each case across all variables. This property is of special importance to disciplines such as psychology, sociology, and anthropology that often describe data in terms of profiles. While a profile is formally defined as nothing more than a vector of attribute values for a case (Sneath and Sokal, 1973) the comparison of each case, as represented by a vector but displayed graphically as a profile, is often the desired end product of a classification. For instance, the MMPI data used in this book are often plotted to create profiles of different individuals (see Figure 1).

One of the major drawbacks of the use of the correlation coefficient as a similarity measure is its sensitivity to shape at the expense of the magnitude of differences between the variables. As first demonstrated by Cronbach and Gleser (1953), the similarity between profiles can be decomposed into three parts: *shape*, the pattern of dips and rises across the variables; *scatter*, the dispersion of the scores around their average; and *elevation* (level or size), the mean score of the case over all of the variables. That the product-moment correlation coefficient is sensitive only to shape means that two profiles can have a correlation of +1.0 and yet not be identical (i.e., the profiles of each case do not pass through the same points). Figure 2 shows two MMPI profiles, one with a solid line and the other with a dashed line. Their shapes are identical. Although the correlation between these two profiles is +1.0, they are not truly identical because one is elevated. Thus, a high correlation can occur between profiles as long as the measurements of one profile are in a linear relationship to another. Some information is lost, therefore, when the correlation coefficient is used, and it is possible that misleading results can be obtained if the effects of dispersion and elevation on profile data are not also considered.

There are other potential limitations of the coefficient. It often fails to satisfy the triangle inequality, and as many have pointed out, the use of the method to calculate the correlation of cases does not make statistical sense, because one must obtain the mean value across different variable types rather than across cases, as in the standard use of the method. The meaning of the "mean" across these variables is far from clear.

Despite these drawbacks, the coefficient has been used successfully in a wide variety of research applications involving cluster analysis. Hamer and Cunningham (1981) have demonstrated that the correlation coefficient is superior in its ability to reduce the total number of misclassifications when used with a consistent clustering method as compared to

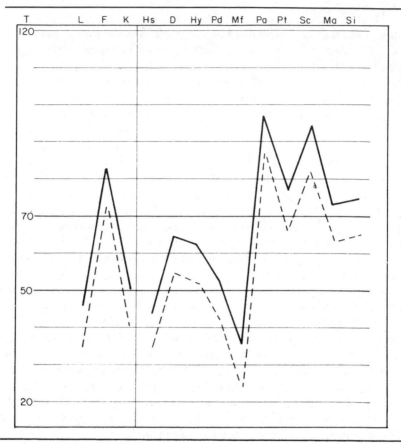

Figure 2: MMPI Profiles (r = 1.0)

other similarity coefficients. Paradoxically, correlation proves to be of value precisely because it is not affected by dispersion and size differences between the variables. Of considerable importance to the success of this study, however, was that the researchers were able to postulate their need for a shape coefficient because they believe that dispersion and size effects on the profile data were created by differences in the experience and judgment of raters of job classifications, and were thus not due to the intrinsic variability of the job classifications themselves.

DISTANCE MEASURES

Because of their intuitive appeal, distance measures have enjoyed widespread popularity. Technically, they are best described as *dissimi-*

larity measures; most of the more popular coefficients demonstrate similarity by high values within their ranges, but distance measures are scaled in the reverse. Two cases are identical if each one is described by variables with the same magnitudes. In this case, the distance between them is zero. Distance measures normally have no upper bounds, and are scale-dependent. Among the more popular representations of distance is Euclidean distance, defined as

$$d_{ij} = \sqrt{\sum_{k=1}^{p} (x_{ik} - x_{jk})^2}$$

where d_{ij} is the distance between cases i and j, and x_{ik} is the value of the kth variable for the ith case. To avoid the use of the square root, the value of distance is often squared, and this is usually indicated by the term d_{ij}^2. As might be expected, this expression is referred to as "squared Euclidean distance."

Other types of distance can be defined, and another popular measure is the Manhattan distance, or city-block metric, which is defined as

$$d_{ij} = \sum_{k=1}^{p} \left| x_{ik} - x_{jk} \right|$$

Other metrics can be defined, but most are specific forms of the special class of metric distance functions known as Minkowski metrics, defined in a general form as

$$d_{ij} = \left(\sum_{k=1}^{p} \left| x_{ik} - x_{jk} \right|^r \right)^{1/r}$$

There are other distances that are not Minkowski metrics, and the most important of these is Mahalanobis D^2, also called generalized distance (Mahalanobis, 1936). This metric is defined as

$$d_{ij} = (X_i - X_j)' \Sigma^{-1} (X_i - X_j)$$

where Σ is the pooled within-groups variance-covariance matrix, and X_i and X_j are vectors of the values of the variables for cases i and j. Unlike Euclidean or other Minkowski metrics, this metric incorporates the correlations among variables by the inclusion of the variance-covariance matrix. When the correlation between variables is zero, Mahalanobis D^2 is equivalent to squared Euclidean distance.

Despite their importance, Euclidean and other distance metrics suffer from serious problems, among the most critical of which is that the estimation of the similarity between cases is strongly affected by elevation differences. Variables with both large size differences and standard deviations can essentially swamp the effects of other variables with smaller absolute sizes and standard deviations. Moreover, distance metrics are also affected by transformations of the scale of measurement of the variables, in that Euclidean distance will not preserve distance rankings (Everitt, 1980). In order to reduce the effect of the relative size of the variables, researchers routinely standardize the variables to unit variance and means of zero before the calculation of distance. As noted above, this type of data transformation may lead to other kinds of problems.

Skinner (1978) has proposed a useful and feasible way in which to use both correlation and Euclidean distance to calculate the similarity of profile data so that it is possible to determine which of the factors (shape, size, and dispersion) have contributed to the estimation of similarity. The basic strategy is similar to that proposed by Guertin (1966), in which correlation is used to create homogeneous groups based on shape, and each shape group is then divided with a distance measure into subgroups with similar size and dispersion characteristics (Skinner, 1978). Skinner's procedure, however, represents a considerable advance over this method in that it develops a composite similarity function that integrates both distance and correlation in a computational strategy that tends to minimize measurement error in estimation of profile similarity.

Since the need to standardize data occurs frequently in applied data analysis, a brief example showing the effects of standardization on correlation and distance may be helpful. The data used to illustrate the problem are four MMPI profiles. Each of these profiles represents a psychotic patient with severe psychopathology.

The initial similarity measure to be used with these four profiles is the Pearson product-moment correlation coefficient. The results are shown below:

	A	B	C	D
A	xxxx	.776	.702	.742
B	(3)	xxxx	.729	.779
C	(6)	(5)	xxxx	.936
D	(4)	(2)	(1)	xxxx

The values of the correlations are shown in the upper triangular half of the matrix. These values show that all four profiles have very similar shapes, but, in particular, profiles C and D are close to being identical (r_{CD} = .936). Shown in the lower triangular portion of the matrix are the rank orderings of the similarity values from the most similar (1) to least similar (6). The significance of the rank orderings will become apparent below.

When Euclidean distances are calculated, the following matrix is obtained:

	A	B	C	D
A	xxxx	266	732	736
B	(2)	xxxx	532	465
C	(5)	(4)	xxxx	144
D	(6)	(3)	(1)	xxxx

Notice how different the scaling of the distance coefficients are when compared to the correlation coefficients. Remember, the values of the distance coefficients have no absolute meanings. Again, patients C and D appear to be the most similar with d_{CD} = 144, but there is no clear indication of exactly how good a value of 144 is. In general, the pattern of similarities appears about the same when using correlation and distance, but differences do exist. In particular, the least similar patients using correlation as the similarity measure were patients A and C (r_{AC} = .702). However, Euclidean distance suggests that patients A and D are the least similar (d_{AD} = 736).

To confuse the picture even more, suppose we decide to standardize the data. (Standardization was actually performed on the basis of statistics from the entire 90 case data set.) If the product-moment correlation is used to assess the similarity of the four profiles after standardization, the similarity matrix is as displayed below:

	A	B	C	D
A	xxxx	.602	.284	.433
B	(2)	xxxx	.367	.584
C	(6)	(5)	xxxx	.804
D	(4)	(3)	(1)	xxxx

Notice how different the values of the correlations appear to be when comparing standardized versus nonstandardized data. With nonstandardized data, r_{AC} = .702, but with standardized data, r_{AC} = .284. In both instances, r_{AC} is the smallest value in the matrix, but on standardized data, the value of the correlation coefficient suggests that patients A and C are not at all similar while with nonstandardized data, the absolute value of the correlation ($r = .706$) suggests that A and C in fact are reasonably similar.

Finally, the dissimilarity matrix below shows the Euclidean distances among the patients using standardized data.

	A	B	C	D
A	xxxx	.704	2.572	2.071
B	(1)	xxxx	2.141	1.304
C	(6)	(5)	xxxx	.870
D	(4)	(3)	(2)	xxxx

Again the values change as a function of standardization. However, since the magnitudes of the value of a Euclidean distance coefficient has no inherent meaning, this change is not particularly important. What is important is the relative change. The most dramatic change is that the Euclidean distance coefficient for the standardized data shows patients A and B to be the most similar pair, while the other three similarity matrices showed patients C and D to be the most similar.

To conclude this brief comparison, it is important to note that all four matrices yielded separate, nonidentical rankings of the similarity values. This point is important because it demonstrates what a dramatic effect the choice of a similarity coefficient and a data transformation can have on the relationships in the resulting similarity matrix.

ASSOCIATION COEFFICIENTS

This type of measure is used to establish similarity between cases described by binary variables. It is easiest to discuss these coefficients by reference to the familiar 2 × 2 association table which 1 refers to the presence of a variable and 0 to its absence.

	1	0
1	a	b
0	c	d

A large number (> 30) of these coefficients have been proposed, and it is unrealistic to attempt to describe comprehensively the full range of these measures. As might be expected, most of these coefficients were first defined in biological systematics, although it is likely that some of the simplest of them have been reinvented in a number of disciplines. Few of the measures have been extensively tested, and many have been dropped because of questionable features. Good references for those interested in these coefficients are Sneath and Sokal (1973), Clifford and Stephenson (1975), and Everitt (1980). There are three measures, however, that have been used extensively and deserve special consideration. These are the simple matching coefficient, Jaccard's coefficient, and Gower's coefficient.

The simple matching coefficient is defined as

$$S = \frac{(a + d)}{(a + b + c + d)}$$

where S is the similarity between the two cases which ranges from 0 to 1. As Sneath and Sokal (1973) note, this coefficient cannot be easily transformed into a metric. However, considerable effort has been devoted to the establishment of approximate confidence limits, one of the few methods of this type so honored (Goodall, 1967). The coefficient takes into account the joint absence of a variable (as indicated in the d cell of the association, matrix).

Jaccard's coefficient, defined as

$$S = a/ (a + b + c),$$

avoids the use of joint absences of a variable in the calculation of similarity (it omits the d cell from consideration). Like the simple matching coefficient, it ranges from 0 to 1. It has seen extensive use in the biological sciences as a result of the debate over the inclusion of so-called negative matches (joint absence of a variable). Biologists have noted that if the simple matching coefficient is used, some cases would appear very similar primarily because they both lacked the same features rather than because the features they did have were shared. In contrast, Jaccard's coefficient is concerned only with features that have positive co-occurrences.

The problem of whether to include negative matches has not apparently been an issue in most social sciences, but the problem has arisen in archaeology. If an object is not found with a burial, its absence may be due to either cultural prescriptions or natural processes of disintegration and attrition. It would be inappropriate to base the estimation of similarity between two burials upon the joint absence of an artifact if it is impossible to know which of the two possible explanations is responsible for its absence.

To provide a brief example comparing the simple matching coefficient and Jaccard's coefficient, six data points from the burial data will be examined.

1	C	M	N	1	0	0	1	0	0	0	0
5	C	F	E	0	0	1	0	0	0	1	0
8	T	M	N	0	1	0	1	1	0	0	0
14	T	F	E	1	0	0	0	1	0	1	0
18	A	M	E	1	1	0	1	1	0	1	1
24	A	F	E	1	0	0	0	1	1	1	0

Consider cases 1 (a male child of nonelite status; i.e., CMN for child, male, nonelite) and 8 (male adolescent of nonelite status, i.e., TMN for teenage, male, nonelite). The 2×2 association matrix of common features between these two cases is

		TMN	
		1	0
CMN	1	1	1
	0	2	4

That is, these two cases have only one shared artifact. However, four artifacts were absent from both burials. Thus,

$$S = .625 \ (= 5/8)$$

However,

$$J = .250 \ (= 1/4)$$

In other words, while the simple matching coefficient suggests that cases CMN and TMN are reasonably similar, Jaccard's coefficient implies they are not. The entire 6×6 similarity matrix using the simple matching coefficient is

	CMN	CFE	TMN	TFE	AME	AFE
CMN	–	.500	.625	.625	.500	.500
CFE		–	.375	.625	.250	.500
TMN			–	.500	.625	.375
TFE				–	.625	.875
AME					–	.500
AFE						–

For Jaccard's coefficient, the similarity matrix is

	CMN	CFE	TMN	TFE	AME	AFE
CMN	–	.000	.250	.250	.333	.200
CFE		–	.000	.250	.143	.200
TMN			–	.200	.500	.166
TFE				–	.500	.750
AME					–	.429
AFE						–

These matrices are reasonably similar. For instance, both matrices suggest that cases TFE, AME, and AFE—the older elite burials— are the most similar. However, differences do exist. The two children, cases CMN and CFE, are totally dissimilar according to Jaccard's coefficient, but appear to be relatively similar according to the simple matching coefficient.

Another feature of these matrices is the number of "ties." With the simple matching coefficient there are five pairs of cases for which S = .625, and six cases where S = .500. In fact, in the fifteen cells of the 6×6 similarity matrix, there are only five (!) unique values of S. As we shall show later, some clustering methods perform poorly when so many ties are present in the similarity matrix.

Gower's coefficient is unique because it permits the simultaneous use of variables of different scales of measurement in the estimation of similarity. Proposed by Gower (1971), it is defined as

$$s_{ij} = \sum_{k=1}^{p} S_{ijk} \Big/ \sum_{k=1}^{p} W_{ijk}$$

where W_{ijk} is a weighting variable valued at 1 if a comparison of variable k is considered valid and 0 if it is not. S_{ijk} is a similarity "score" based upon the outcome of the comparison of variable k across cases i and j. In the case of binary variables, W_{ijk} is zero when variable k is not known for one or both individuals under comparison (Everitt, 1980). In the case of so-called negative matches, W_{ijk} is also set to zero. It should be clear that if the data are all binary, the coefficient is identical to Jaccard's.

To demonstrate how this coefficient works, the burial data set has been modified to include two new variable types: stature (measured in centimeters, thus a quantitative variable) and estimated energy expenditure in grave construction or excavation (measured on an ordinal scale with ranks 1, 2, and 3, or low, moderate, and high, respectively). Four cases have been modified:

1	C	M	N	1	0	0	1	0	0	0	0	69	1
7	T	M	N	1	1	0	1	0	0	0	0	167	2
18	A	F	E	1	1	0	1	1	0	1	1	179	3
25	A	M	E	1	0	0	0	1	1	1	1	158	3

For binary data, S_{ijk} is calculated according to the following scoring system:

case i		1	1	0	0
case j		1	0	1	0
score	S_{ijk}	1	0	0	0
weight	W_{ijk}	1	1	1	0

For ordinal data, $S_{ijk} = 1$ when the values of the comparison are identical, and 0 when they are not. Finally, for quantitative data, the equation

$$S_{ijk} = 1 - |x_{ik} - x_{jk}|/R_k$$

where x_{ik} is the score of case i on variable k and R_k is the range of variable k. The resulting similarity matrix from these manipulations for the four cases is

	CMN	TMN	AME	AFE
CMN	–	.527	.285	.170
TMN	–	–	.554	.239
AME	–	–	–	.726
AFE	–	–	–	–

The coefficient has a number of appealing features beyond its ability to accommodate mixed data types. These include its metric qualities and its flexibility, in that the method can be easily modified to include negative matches in the estimation of similarity by simply modifying the binary weighting system. That the coefficient has seen relatively little use in the social sciences can probably be attributed to its failure to appear in any major clustering software packages (see Chapter 5).

PROBABILISTIC SIMILARITY COEFFICIENTS

Coefficients of this type are radically different from those described above in that, technically, the similarity between two cases is not actually calculated. Instead, this type of measure works directly upon the raw data. When forming clusters, the information gain (in the Shannon sense) of the combination of two cases is evaluated, and that combination of cases that provides the least information gain is fused. Another important point about probabilistic measures is that they can be used only with binary data. No workable schemes for using this type of measure with quantitative and qualitative variables has yet been developed. These coefficients have not yet appeared in the social sciences, but they have been used extensively by numerical taxonomists and ecologists for at least a decade. Comprehensive summaries of these measures can be found in Sneath and Sokal (1973) and Clifford and Stephenson (1975).

Suggested Readings

The most valuable and detailed discussion of similarity coefficients relevant to cluster analysis can be found in Sneath and Sokal (1973). These authors devote 74 pages to the discussion of similarity and provide formulae for most of the measures they discuss. Clifford and Stephenson (1975) also provide a useful discussion of similarity measures of relevance to cluster analysis.

More broadly, the theoretical issues associated with similarity are discussed in Hartigan (1967) and Tversky (1977). Skinner's (1978) discussion of shape, elevation, and scatter are very relevant to many uses of similarity measures in social science research. The last three references are important because the concept of similarity is crucial to the formation of clusters. Clusters, after all, are usually defined as groups of *similar* entities. Although most discussions of cluster analysis emphasize the procedures for creating clusters, the choice of a measure of similarity is crucial in any clustering study.

3. A REVIEW OF CLUSTERING METHODS

On the Nature of Clusters

The primary reason for the use of cluster analysis is to find groups of similar entities in a sample of data. These groups are conveniently referred to as clusters. There is no standard or even useful definition of the term "cluster," and many have argued that it is either too late or irrelevant to create one (Bonner, 1964). Despite the lack of a consistent definition of the term, it is clear that clusters have certain properties. Sneath and Sokal (1973) have described a number of these properties, the most important of which are density, variance, dimension, shape, and separation. Although Sneath and Sokal discuss these properties in the context of a metric space, it is obvious (as they acknowledge) that these properties can be logically extended to nonmetric spaces.

Density is a property of a cluster that defines it as a relatively thick swarm of data points in a space when compared to other areas of the space that may have comparatively few or no points. There is no absolute measure of density, but the concept is intuitively obvious. Variance is the degree of dispersion of the points in this space from the center of the cluster. While the analogy of this property with that drawn from statistical inference is valid, the researcher should remember that clusters do not necessarily represent multivariate normal populations. In this context, it is best to view the property of variance as one that simply describes the relative nearness of points to one another in the space. Therefore, clusters can be said to be "tight" when all data points are near the centroid, or they may be "loose" when the data points are dispersed from the center. Dimension is a property closely related to that of variance; if a cluster can be identified, it is then possible to measure its "radius." This property is useful only if the clusters under consideration form hyperspheres (i.e., have a round shape) in the multidimensional space described by the variables.

Shape is simply the arrangement of points in the space. While the typical conception of the shape of clusters is that they are hyperspheres or ellipsoids, many different kinds of shapes, such as elongated clusters, are possible. If clusters are shaped in this manner, the concept of a radius or diameter is not useful. Instead, the "connectivity" of the points in the cluster, a relative measure of the distance between them, can be calculated. If clusters are of other, more bizarre, shapes such as those shown by Everitt (1980), the concept of connectivity is somewhat less useful, and relative estimates of diameter and density therefore have less meaning. Separation is the degree to which clusters overlap or lie apart in the space. For instance, clusters may be relatively close to one another with no clear boundaries or they may be widely separated with large gaps between them.

Taken together, these terms can be used to describe any type of clusters within a space. Following Everitt (1980), clusters are "continuous regions of (a) space containing a relatively high density of points, separated from other such regions by regions containing a relatively low density of points." The importance of this definition is that it does not restrict the conceptualization of clusters to any particular form before data analysis takes place.

Seven major families of clustering methods have been developed:

(1) hierarchical agglomerative,

(2) hierarchical divisive,

(3) iterative partitioning,

(4) density search,

(5) factor analytic,

(6) clumping, and

(7) graph theoretic.

Each of these families represents a different perspective on the creation of groups, and the results obtained when different methods are applied to the same data can be very different. Certain families of methods have been found to be particularly useful in specific sciences. Hierarchical agglomerative methods are most frequently used in the biological sciences, whereas factor analytic methods have been popular in psychology. What is important to remember when faced with the difficult choice of which clustering method to use is that the method must be compatible with the desired nature of the classification, the variables to be used, and the similarity measure used to estimate the resemblance between cases if one is required.

The three most popular families of clustering methods used in the social sciences are hierarchical agglomerative, iterative partitioning, and factor analytic. Because of their prominence, each of these three is described in some detail, and each is illustrated through the use of the two data sets described in Chapter 1. The other, less-known families are more briefly discussed.

Hierarchical Agglomerative Methods

Hierarchical agglomerative methods have been dominant among the seven families of methods in terms of the frequency of their applied use. In a review of all published articles using cluster analysis during 1973, Blashfield and Aldenderfer (1978b) found that two-thirds of these articles presented the use of some hierarchical agglomerative method.

The easiest hierarchical agglomerative method to understand is *single linkage*. Consider the 6 × 6 similarity matrix using Jaccard's coefficient that was presented for the burial data in Chapter 2. Single linkage begins the clustering process by searching for the two most similar entities in the matrix. In this example, the most similar cases are TFE (teenage, female, elite) and AFE (adult, female, elite), that are joined at the J = .750 level of similarity. At the next step, case AME is also joined to this group because it has a similarity of .500 with case TFE. This occurs because under the linkage rule defined for single linkage, a new candidate for cluster membership can be joined to an existing group on the basis of the highest level of similarity of any member of the existing group. That is, only a "single link" is required between two cases for them to merge. The third step is to join case TMN to the cluster containing cases AFE, AME, and TFE because it also has a similarity of .500 with case AME. The fourth step in the clustering process joins case CMN to the group composed of cases TFE, AME, AFE, and TMN at the J = .333 level of similarity. The fifth and final step joins case CFE to the rest at the J = .250 level of similarity.

Four important observations about hierarchical agglomerative methods can be derived from this example. First, these methods all search for N × N similarity matrix (where N refers to the number of entities) and sequentially merge the most similar cases. That is, these methods are agglomerative. The second important point to note is that the sequence of mergers of clusters can be represented visually by a tree diagram, often called a dendrogram. The tree diagram for the single linkage results on the six burial data points is shown in Figure 3. Each step where a pair of cases was merged is represented as a branch in this tree. Note that this tree portrays a hierarchical organization to the relations between the six data points. At the lowest level, all six are independent; at the next level, they have been merged into one group and three independent cases; finally, at the highest level, they are joined into one large group.

The third major point is that they all require exactly N − 1 steps to cluster a similarity matrix. On the first step, all cases are treated as individual clusters. At the final step, all cases are merged into one large group.

Finally, hierarchical agglomerative methods are conceptually simple to understand. Single linkage does not require an understanding of matrix algebra or an extensive background in multivariate statistics. Instead, the method is based on a simple rule of how to search a similarity matrix and when to combine cases. Although other hierarchical agglomerative methods are slightly more complex, they are all relatively simple and reflect different possible merger rules (called linkage forms in most of this literature). By definition, these clustering methods produce nonoverlapping clusters. These clusters, however, are

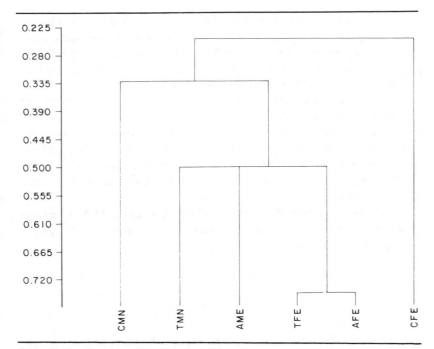

Figure 3: Dendrogram of Six-Case Burial Data Set

nested, in that each cluster can be subsumed as a member of a larger, more inclusive cluster at a higher level of similarity. The most familiar expression of the results of these clustering methods is the dendrogram (tree diagram) which is a graphical display of the hierarchical structure implied by the similarity matrix and clustered by the linkage rule.

Despite the simplicity of these methods, they suffer from a number of problems. Unless special algorithms are employed, hierarchical methods require the calculation and storage of a potentially large similarity matrix. The storage of this matrix effectively places an upper limit on the number of cases that can be clustered. For example, a data set with 500 cases would require the storage and the repeated searching of a matrix with almost 125,000 values. Another problem with these methods is that they make only one pass through the data, and a poor early partition of the data set cannot be modified in subsequent steps of the clustering process (Gower, 1967). A third problem with most of these methods (except single linkage) is that they can generate different solutions simply by reordering the data in the similarity matrix, and they also are not stable when cases are dropped out of the analysis. Stability is an important property of any classification in that stable groups are more likely to represent "natural" groups in the data than those that disappear when cases are reordered or a few cases are omitted. The problem of stability is especially pertinent when dealing with small samples of cases (Jardine and Sibson, 1971).

Hierarchical agglomerative methods are distinguished primarily by their different rules for the formation of clusters. Some authors use the term "sorting strategy" to refer to linkage form. There are many possible linkage rules, each yielding a unique hierarchical method. While at least twelve different linkage forms have been proposed, four have become widely popular: single linkage, complete linkage, average linkage, and Ward's method.

Lance and Williams (1967) have developed a formula that can be used to describe linkage rules in a general form for any hierarchical agglomerative method. The rule is defined as

$$d(h,k) = A(i) \cdot d(h,i) + A(j) \cdot d(h,j) + B \cdot d(i,j)$$
$$+ C \cdot ABS(d(h,i) - d(h,j))$$

where $d(h,k)$ is the dissimilarity of distance between cluster h and cluster k, where cluster k is the result of combining clusters (or cases) i and j during an agglomerative step. This formula provides a method for calculating the distance between some object (h) and a new cluster (K) that is formed by the merger of objects i and j into a common cluster. The capital letters refer to parameters that further define the linkage form; in single linkage, for instance, the values of the parameters are $A(i) = A(j) = \frac{1}{2}$; $B = O$; and $C = \frac{1}{2}$. This formula has proven to be of great help in developing computational algorithms for these methods.

To illustrate the operation of hierarchical methods, and to show the effects of different linkage rules, the four most popular methods have been used to cluster the MMPI data set.

Single linkage. This method, described by Sneath (1957), forms clusters by the following rule: Cases will be joined to existing clusters if at least one of the members of the existing cluster is of the same level of similarity as the case under consideration for inclusion. Connections are thus based solely upon single links between cases and clusters. The major advantage of this method is its desirable mathematical properties: It is invariant to monotonic transformations of the similarity matrix, and it is unaffected by ties in the data (Jardine and Sibson, 1971). The first of these properties, invariance under monotonic transformations, is quite important since almost all other hierarchical agglomerative

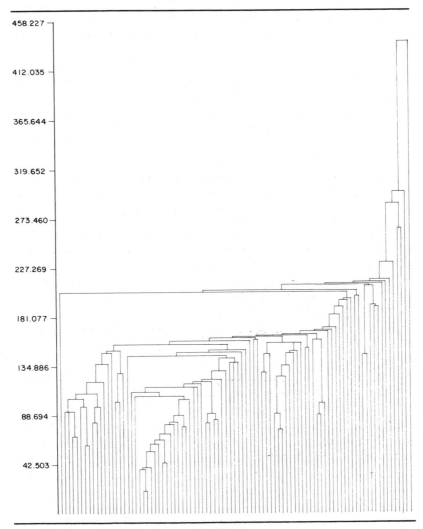

Figure 4: Single Linkage Dendrogram, MMPI Data

methods do not have this property. This means that single linkage is one
of the few methods that will not be affected by any data transformation
that retains the same relative ordering of values in the similarity matrix.

The major drawback of single linkage, however, is that it has been
shown in practice to have a tendency to chain, or form long, elongated
clusters. An example of chaining can be shown in the tree diagram for
the MMPI data (Figure 4). Notice that toward the end of the clustering
process, one large cluster has been formed, and the remaining cases are

added, one by one, to the large cluster. The two-cluster solution as found by single linkage has the trivial result of containing one cluster with 89 cases and one cluster of one case.

A few other points of interest can be noted in Figure 4. First, a visual examination of the figure does not suggest how many clusters exist in the data. In contrast, the tree diagram from complete linkage (Figure 5) strongly suggests the presence of two clusters. Second, the diagnostic labels associated with the MMPI profiles are not clearly grouped in the figure. There is a collection of neurotic (N) profiles on the left side of the tree and a collection of character disorder (CD) profiles in the middle. The remainder of the tree is a mixed bag of P (psychotic), N, and a few CD profiles. In short, single linkage has not generated a solution that accurately recovers the known structure of the data.

Complete linkage. This method is the logical opposite of single linkage clustering in that the linkage rule states that any candidate for inclusion into an existing cluster must be within a certain level of similarity to *all* members of that cluster (Sokal and Michener, 1958). This is certainly a more rigorous rule than that embodied in single linkage, and, therefore, complete linkage has a tendency to find relatively compact, hyperspherical clusters composed of highly similar cases. Although the tree resulting from complete linkage (Figure 5) does give a clear sense of clusters in the data, the comparison of the cluster memberships generated by complete linkage to the known structure does not show high concordance. The information shown below represents the membership overlap between the clusters and the diagnostic categories. A perfect solution would have a one-to-one correspondence of clusters and diagnostic categories. This clearly does not obtain in the complete linkage solution.

		Clusters		
		I	II	III
	N	10	0	20
Diagnoses	P	15	13	2
	CD	8	4	18

Average linkage. Proposed by Sokal and Michener (1958), average linkage clustering was developed as an antidote to the extremes of both single and complete linkage. Although there are a number of variants of the method, each essentially computes an average of the similarity of a case under consideration with all cases in the existing cluster and, subsequently, joins the case to that cluster if a given level of similarity is

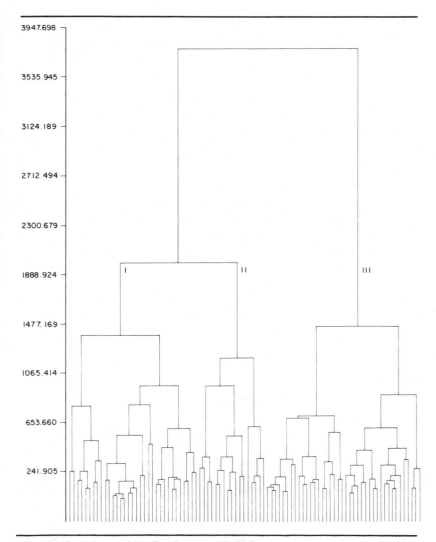

Figure 5: Complete Linkage Dendrogram, MMPI Data

achieved using this average value. The most commonly used variant of average linkage computes the arithmetic average of similarities among the cases. Other variants of average linkage are designed to calculate the similarity between the centroids of two clusters that might be merged. Average linkage has been used extensively in the biological sciences, but has only recently begun to see much use in the social sciences.

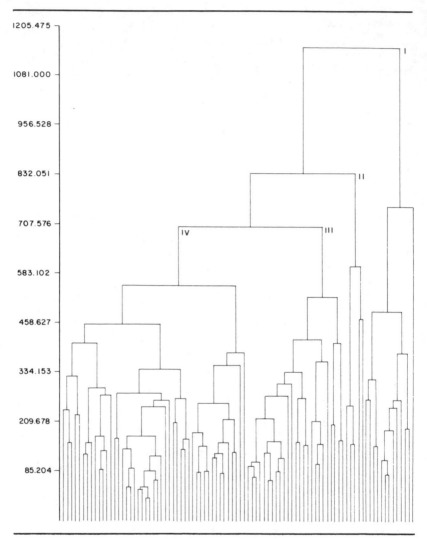

Figure 6: Average Linkage Dendrogram, MMPI Data

Examination of Figure 6 shows an interesting relationship between the tree generated by average linkage and the known diagnostic classes. The first cluster (I) contains almost half of the psychotic profiles. The second cluster (II) is quite small and is evenly divided into neurotic and psychotic profiles. The third cluster (III) contains virtually all of the neurotic cases, while the fourth (IV) and largest cluster is the entire collection of character disorder profiles plus many of the psychotic profiles. The overlap of clusters and diagnostic categories is shown below.

		Clusters			
		I	II	III	IV
	N	0	2	26	2
Diagnoses	P	13	3	0	14
	CD	0	0	0	30

Ward's method. This method is designed to optimize the minimum variance within clusters (Ward, 1963). This objective function is also known as the within-groups sum of squares or the error sum of squares (ESS). The formula for the error sum of squares is

$$ESS = x_i^2 - 1/n(\Sigma x_i)^2$$

where x_i is the score of the ith case. At the first step of the clustering process, when each case is in its own cluster, the ESS is 0. The method works by joining those groups or cases that result in the minimum increase in the ESS. The method tends to find (or create) clusters of relatively equal sizes and shapes as hyperspheres. Ward's method has been virtually ignored in the biological sciences, but it has been widely used in many of the social sciences (Blashfield, 1980).

The tree from Ward's method (Figure 7) shows a clear three-cluster solution. As with average linkage, there is an organized relationship between the clusters and the diagnostic categories, but Ward's method does not generate a perfect solution. The membership overlap is shown below.

		Clusters		
		I	II	III
	N	29	1	0
Diagnoses	P	1	16	13
	CD	0	30	0

A common problem associated with the use of Ward's method is that the clusters found by this method can be ordered in terms of their overall elevation. For instance, in this solution, cluster III has the most elevated profile, while cluster II is the least elevated. Practical applications of

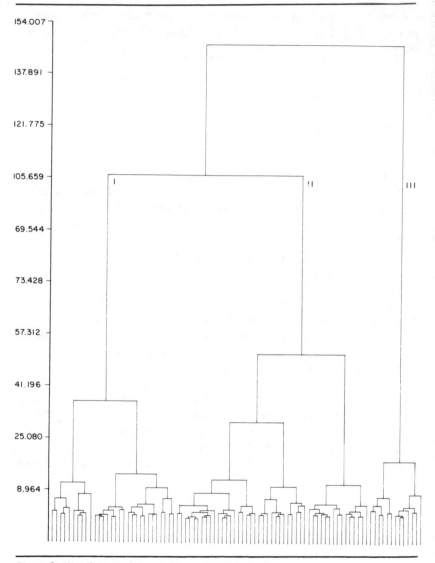

Figure 7: Ward's Method Dendrogram, MMPI Data

Ward's method in social science research have shown it to generate solutions that are heavily influenced by profile elevation.

There are a number of ways to compare the various hierarchical agglomerative methods. One is to analyze how these methods transform the relationships between the points in the multivariate space. Space-contracting methods affect these relationships by "reducing" the space between any groups in the data. When new points are encountered in the space by this type of method, they tend to be joined to existing groups rather than to be used to start new clusters. Space-dilating linkage forms are the opposite. Clusters here appear to "recede" on formation; thus smaller, more "distinct"clusters are formed in that space. This strategy of linkage also tends to create clusters of hyperspherical form and roughly equivalent size. Complete linkage and Ward's method are said to be space-dilating. Finally, space-conserving methods, such as average linkage, are said to maintain the nature of the original space.

To some authors, such as Williams et al. (1971), the properties of space-contracting methods are seen as flaws, especially in applied data analysis, whereas to others—most notably Jardine and Sibson (1968)—these methods are to be preferred because of their desirable mathematical properties regardless of their practical outcome. Everitt (1980) balances these two extremes by noting that the success of these types of methods in data analysis depends greatly on the a priori conception of what types of clusters are expected and the actual structure of the data. The real problem, as will be discussed at length in a later chapter, is to determine when one of these strategies has imposed an inappropriate structure on the data.

Iterative Partitioning Methods

Unlike hierarchical agglomerative methods, iterative partitioning methods of cluster analysis have not been extensively used or examined, and many of the important features of their operation are not well understood by potential users. Briefly, most partitioning methods work in the following fashion:

(1) Begin with an initial partition of the data set into some specified number of clusters; compute the centroids of these clusters.

(2) Allocate each data point to the cluster that has the nearest centroid.

(3) Compute the new centroids of the clusters; clusters are not updated until there has been a complete pass through the data.

(4) Alternate steps 2 and 3 until no data points change clusters (Anderberg, 1973).

The MMPI data have been clustered with the k-means procedure of CLUSTAN (Wishart, 1982) to demonstrate the basic features of iterative methods. The first step is to form an initial partition of the data. CLUSTAN does this by arbitrarily assigning the 90 cases into three clusters (k = 3). The value of k is user-specified. Then the centroids of the clusters are computed.

Next, the Euclidean distances are calculated between all cases and the three-cluster centroids, and then the cases are assigned to the nearest centroids. For the MMPI data, this means that 51 cases are moved from the cluster in which they have been placed initially to a cluster with a nearer centroid. After all reassignments, the centroids of the new clusters are computed. These centroids are quite different and approximate the actual three groups in the MMPI data. The second step is repeated, in this case involving eight reassignments. New centroids are computed, and another pass is instituted. In the third pass, no reassignments occur. All cases at this point are assigned to the nearest cluster centroids.

Unlike hierarchical agglomerative methods, which require the calculation and storage of an N × N matrix of similarities between cases, iterative methods work directly upon the raw data. They therefore offer the opportunity of handling distinctly larger data sets than hierarchical methods. Moreover, iterative methods make more than one pass through the data and can compensate for a poor initial partition of the data, thereby avoiding one of the major drawbacks of hierarchical agglomerative methods. These methods also produce single-rank clusters that are not nested and therefore are not part of a hierarchy. Most iterative methods do not permit overlapping clusters.

Despite these attractive features, iterative partitioning methods suffer from one major limitation. The most straightforward way to discover the optimal partition of a data set by means of an iterative method is to form all possible partitions of that data set. This seemingly simple solution, except for the smallest and most trivial of problems, is computationally impossible. For 15 cases and 3 clusters, this approach requires the examination of 217,945,728,000 unique partitions, clearly beyond the capacity of modern computers.

Since all possible partitions of even small data sets cannot be examined, researchers have developed a wide range of heuristic procedures that can be used to sample a small subset of all possible partitions of a data set in hope of finding, or at least approximating, the optimal partition of a data set. This situation is similar to that encountered with the heuristic approach to the development of linkage rules for hierarchical agglomerative methods; the sampling procedures are reasonable and plausible, but few, if any, are based upon a comprehensive body of statistical theory or reasoning.

Most of the heuristic, computational, and statistical properties of iterative partitioning methods can be summarized by reference to three major factors: (1) choice of initial partition, (2) type of pass, and (3) statistical criterion. These three factors have been combined in a bewildering variety of ways to produce algorithms to sample data to find the optimal partition. Not surprisingly, different combinations of these factors have led to the development of methods that produce different results when applied to the same data.

(1) *Initial partition.* There are two basic ways to start an iterative method: the definition of seed points or the selection of an appropriate starting partition. Seed points are estimates of cluster centroids (Anderberg, 1973). When seed points are used, the data points are assigned to the nearest cluster centroid on the first pass through the data. Starting partitions involve the specification of the first cluster assignment. In this procedure, the centroids of each cluster are defined as the multivariate mean of the cases within a cluster. Starting partitions can be chosen randomly, as in the example with the MMPI data, or they can be determined by the user in some fashion (e.g., the user can select a hierarchical clustering solution as the initial partition of the data).

(2) *Type of pass.* This factor is concerned with the way in which cases are assigned to clusters; again, there are two basic types: k-means passes and hill climbing passes.

K-means passes, also referred to as the "nearest centroid sorting pass" and the "reassignment pass," simply involve the reassignment of cases to the cluster with the nearest centroid. K-means passes can be either combinatorial or noncombinatorial. The former method requires the recalculation of the centroid of a cluster after each change in its membership, while the latter recalculates the cluster centroid only after an entire pass through the data has been completed. One other important distinction is that k-means passes can also be either exclusive or inclusive. Exclusive methods remove the case under consideration from the parent cluster when a centroid is computed, whereas inclusive methods include them.

Hill climbing passes, rather than assigning cases to a cluster on the basis of the distance of that case from the centroid of a cluster, move cases about on the basis of whether or not the proposed move optimizes the value of a particular statistical criterion.

(3)*Statistical criterion.* Those methods based upon hill climbing passes use one or more of the following criteria: $\text{tr}W$, $\text{tr}W^{-1}B$, $\det W$, and the largest eigenvalue of $W^{-1}B$, where W refers to the pooled within-cluster covariance matrix and B is the pooled between-cluster covariance matrix. Each of these statistics is often discussed in multivariate analysis of variance (MANOVA), and the logic of their use derives from the statistical theory associated with MANOVA. In effect, all four criteria are concerned with detecting the homogeneity of clusters represented in a multivariate space. Although k-means methods do not explicitly use a statistical criterion to move cases, they implicitly optimize the trW criterion. That is, a k-means procedure attempts to minimize the variance within each cluster. It is important to note, however, that an iterative k-means pass and a hill climbing pass using the trW criterion will produce different results when applied to the same data.

Like hierarchical agglomerative methods, each of these statistical criteria finds a certain type of cluster. The trW criterion is biased in favor of hyperspherical, very homogeneous clusters. More important, this criterion can be markedly affected by simple transformations of the raw data, such as standardization. Det W is not transformation or scale-dependent and, furthermore, does not assume that clusters are hyperspherical. It does, however, assume that the clusters are of the same shape, and this may cause some difficulty in applied data analysis. Scott and Symons (1971) have shown that the criterion has a tendency to create clusters of roughly equal size even if such clusters are not present in the data. Unfortunately, the characteristics of the other criteria are not well understood because they have not been studied or extensively compared.

One major problem shared by all iterative methods is the problem of suboptimal solutions. Since these methods can sample only a very small proportion of all possible partitions of a data set, there is some possibility that a suboptimal partition may be chosen. This has also been referred to as the problem of local (as opposed to global) optima. Unfortunately, there is really no objective way to determine if a solution obtained from an iterative partitioning method is globally optimal; one avenue to the solution of the problem, however, is to use the clustering method in conjunction with an appropriate validation procedure (see Chapter 4).

Monte Carlo studies of the performance of iterative methods have shown that the major cause of suboptimal solutions is a poor starting partition of the data set (Blashfield and Aldenderfer, 1978a; Milligan, 1980). The k-means pass is extremely sensitive to poor initial partitions, and the problem is exacerbated by the selection of a random initial partition, a popular option with much iterative software. Blashfield and Aldenderfer (1978a) have shown that a rational selection of the starting partition did little to improve this situation, but Milligan (1980) has demonstrated that the k-means pass, using an initial starting partition derived from average linkage clustering, provided superior recovery of known data structure when compared to the performance of other iterative and hierarchical clustering methods. Others have suggested that iterative methods produce optimal solutions regardless of the starting partition if the data are well structured (Everitt, 1980; Bayne et al., 1980), but, clearly, more Monte Carlo work is needed to resolve this problem.

Factor Analysis Variants

These methods of cluster analysis have achieved considerable popularity in psychology, and most of the methods are known as factor analysis variants, inverse factor analysis, or Q-type factoring. These methods start by forming a correlation matrix of similarities among cases. Conventionally, factor analysis is performed on a $P \times P$ correlation matrix, but when used to define clusters, it is performed on the $N \times N$ correlation matrix. Factors are extracted from the correlation matrix, and the cases are assigned to clusters based on their factor loadings.

The use of Q-type factor analysis has a lengthy and stormy history. The strongest recent proponents of this type of clustering have been Overall and Klett (1972) and Skinner (1979). Criticisms of factor analytic methods of clustering include the implausible use of a linear model across cases, the problem of multiple factor loadings (what is to be done with a case that has high loadings on more than one factor), and the double centering of the data (Everitt, 1980; Fleiss et al., 1971).

To give the reader an idea about how inverse factor analysis is used, an example will be provided using Modal Profile Analysis (Skinner, 1979). This clustering method uses the Eckert-Young decomposition technique to form a low dimensional space that can represent relationships among entities. Skinner's approach to dimensional versus categorical models of classification, a conceptual issue often raised when inverse factor analysis is mentioned, is discussed in journal article by Skinner (1979). The program has three major steps: (1) initial estimation of the types, (2) replication of the types across multiple samples, and (3) testing the generality of the types on a new sample. The first step of this procedure is illustrated with the MMPI data.

A three-type solution was selected since we know a priori that three clusters exist in the data. The first seven eigenvalues[2] of the solution were

$$28.07$$
$$17.16$$
$$11.49$$
$$9.39$$
$$5.39$$
$$4.60$$
$$4.22$$

Using standard factor analysis interpretations of how to estimate the number of factors, one might argure that a two-type or four-type solution would be more reasonable that a three-type solution. Nonetheless, since we knew how many diagnostic categories actually existed in the data, only the three-cluster solution was examined.

The first type to result from Modal Profile Analysis was a bipolar dimension that was positively correlated with the neurotic patients and negatively correlated with the character disorder patients. The third type primarily contained the psychotic patients. The second factor was a mixture of patients from all three groups.

The three modal profiles are similar to what most clinical psychologists would describe as typical MMPI profiles of "neurotic," "character disorder," or "psychotic" patients. However, they are less extreme than the mean profiles for the actual three groups in the data. This is consistent with the focus of inverse factor analysis, which emphasizes profile shape rather than elevation.

Other Methods

Hierarchical divisive methods are the logical opposites of agglomerative methods. Here, all entities belong to one cluster at the beginning of the procedure (i.e., $K = 1$), and then this encompassing cluster is cut into successively smaller chunks. There are two divisive strategies: monothetic and polythetic. A monothetic cluster is a group in which all entities have approximately the same value on a particular variable. Thus, monothetic clusters are defined by certain variables on which certain scores are *necessary* for membership in these clusters. In contrast, polythetic clusters are groups of entities for which no single variable is necessary, but certain subsets of the variables are *sufficient* for membership to the clusters. All three—hierarchical, agglomerative, and iterative partitioning—methods will form only polythetic clusters.

Monothetic divisive strategies are used primarily with binary data, and the procedure used to divide the population of cases into subgroups is based upon the identification of a variable that maximizes the dissimilarity between the resulting clusters. The most commonly used divisive criteria are based upon the chi-square statistic or some type of information statistic (Clifford and Stephenson, 1975; Everitt, 1980). The monothetic approach to divisive clustering, also known as association analysis, has been used extensively in ecology, but the use of the method in the social sciences has been limited to archaeology (Peebles, 1972; Whallon, 1971, 1972).

Density search methods are natural outgrowths of the concept that views a cluster as a region of a "high" density of points in a space relative to those regions surrounding it. These methods essentially "search" the space for natural modes in the data that represent these areas of high density. Two basic strategies of density search methods are methods based upon a variant of single linkage clustering and methods based upon mixtures of multivariate probability distributions.

As Everitt (1980) notes, density search methods based upon single linkage clustering have been developed as antidotes to the now-familiar problem of chaining. Unlike single linkage, density search methods have stringent rules that serve to initiate new clusters rather than joining newly encountered entities to already existing groups. Typically these rules are based upon a measurement of distance from an existing cluster to a new case or cluster, such as in mode analysis (Wishart, 1969), or by a measure of average similarity in the TAXMAP method proposed by Carmichael and Sneath (1969). Mergers between cases and clusters are not made if the rule is not satisfied. The most widely used of these methods is mode analysis, first proposed by Wishart (1969) and subsequently incorporated into the CLUSTAN suite of cluster analysis programs (Wishart, 1982). Despite its intuitive appeal, the method does suffer from some drawbacks, the most prominent of which is its scale-dependence. Furthermore, the method is based upon the assumption that the clusters sought in the space are spherical.

The other major group of density search methods are those that attempt to discover the parameters of mixtures. A mixture is defined as a collection of samples representing different populations of entities. For instance, the MMPI data set is a mixture because it contains samples from three different populations: neurotics, psychotics, and character disorders. This approach to cluster analysis is clearly based upon a statistical model that assumes that members of different groups or classes should have different probability distributions of variables. The goal of clustering these data is to define the parameters of the underlying populations.

By far the most important of those methods that seek to resolve mixtures are the NORMIX and NORMAP procedures developed by Wolfe (1970, 1971). NORMIX obtains maximum likelihood estimates of the parameters of multivariate normal mixtures of distributions. This method assumes that the means and covariance structures of the underlying populations are different; the NORMAP procedure makes the simpler assumption that the within-groups covariance structures are the same. Both NORMIX and NORMAP are unique in that they do not assign entities to particular clusters but instead give the probability of membership of each case to every cluster estimated. For instance, in the case of overlapping clusters, a probability of 0.5 for the membership of a case in the two overlapping clusters would be obtained (Wishart, 1982).

These methods are particularly sensitive to the problem of suboptimal solutions (Everitt, 1980), because in general there may be more than one solution to a maximum likelihood equation. While it is possible to compare the estimates for different nonoptimal solutions, this is not easy and may not be feasible for even moderately sized problems. A further drawback to these methods is that they are based upon the assumption that all underlying mixtures are formed from the multivariate normal distribution. It is obvious that other types of distributions are likely, and it is not clear how robust these methods are to the violation of this assumption.

Clumping methods are unique in that they permit the creation of overlapping clusters. Unlike hierarchical methods, this family of clustering methods does not produce hierarchical classifications; instead, cases are permitted to be members of more than one cluster. Most of the early development of these methods was stimulated by linguistic research, because in this field it is important to represent words as having multiple meanings.

These methods require the calculation of a similarity matrix between the cases and work by attempting to optimize the value of a statistical criterion technically referred to as a "cohesion function." Items are then iteratively reallocated until the function to be optimized is stable. Because the methods create only two groups at a time, the methods usually partition the data by random methods into a number of different starting configurations, each of which can be analyzed for its utility. A serious problem with these methods is that because of this awkward search procedure, the same groups are often repeatedly discovered, thus providing no new information. Another practical problem is that since these methods have not been used extensively, their characteristics are not well known. Jardine and Sibson (1968) have proposed a clumping method based upon graph theory, which, while it avoids the serious problem of the repetitious discovery of groups, is limited to the analysis of extremely small groups ($N \leq 25$) due to extreme computational demands (see also Cole and Wishart, 1970).

In many ways, graph theoretic methods are among the most innovative methods available. Of considerable interest to the theoretician, if not the user, is that the clustering methods in this family are based upon the well-developed theorems and axioms of graph theory. The importance of this is that since the theorems of graph theory have powerful deductive fertility, it is possible that the theory may provide an alternative to the predominately heuristic status of other clustering methods. For instance, hierarchical agglomerative clustering methods can be described succinctly in graph theoretic terms (Dubes and Jain, 1980). Graph theory has also led to the creation of a null hypothesis that can be used to test for the presence of clusters in a similarity matrix. This is known as the Random Graph Hypothesis, which simply states that all rank-order proximity matrices are equally likely (Ling, 1975). Graph theory has also contributed to the development of more effective computational algorithms for popular clustering methods and has in some instances permitted the maximum number of cases to be analyzed to be quite large.

Determining the Number of Clusters

Since cluster analysis is designed to create homogeneous groups, it is only natural to consider those procedures that can be used to determine just how many groups are present in the results of a clustering study. For instance, the nested tree structure of a dendrogram suggests that many different groups may be present in the data, and the obvious question is where to "cut" the tree so that the optimal number of groups is found. Similarly, iterative methods require the user to specify the number of groups present in the data prior to the creation of these groups by the procedure.

Unfortunately, this fundamental step is among the as yet unsolved problems of cluster analysis (Everitt, 1979). The two most important reasons that little progress has been made toward the solution of the problem are the lack of a suitable null hypothesis and the complex nature of multivariate sampling distributions.

Much of the difficulty in creating a workable null hypothesis has been the lack of a consistent and comprehensive definition of the structure and content of a cluster, but, as we have pointed out elsewhere, this definition is not likely to be forthcoming. The concept of "no structure" in a data set (one possible null hypothesis) is far from clear, and it is not obvious what types of tests could be devised to determine if structure is or is not present. Those null hypotheses that have been established— such as the random graph hypothesis and the random position hypothesis—while potentially useful, are extremely limited in scope and have yet to be applied in practical data analysis (Dubes and Jain, 1980). In any case, as Dubes and Jain continue,

> a rejection of the null hypothesis is not particularly significant because meaningful alternative hypotheses have not been developed; a practical and mathematically useful definition of "clustering structure" does not yet exist.

Equally intractable is the problem of the mixture of potentially complex multivariate sampling distributions in the analysis of real-world data. Although many aspects of multivariate normal distributions are well understood, it is not reasonable to expect real-world data to conform to this standard; furthermore, many samples of real-world data are composed of complex mixtures of different multivariate sampling distributions of unknown structure. Since no body of distributional or statistical theory exists to unravel these mixtures, it is also unreasonable to assume that formal tests of clustering tendency are likely to be developed.

The response to these constraints has been mixed. In some fields, most notably the biological sciences, the problem of defining the number of clusters present has not been of paramount importance simply because the goal of the analysis is to explore the general pattern of the relationships between entities as represented by a hierarchical tree. In the social sciences, however, two basic approaches to determining the number of clusters present have evolved: heuristic procedures and formal tests.

Heuristic procedures are by far the most commonly used methods. At the most basic level, a hierarchical tree is "cut" by the subjective inspection of the different levels of the tree. For the dendrogram in Figure 8, a Ward's method solution of the full burial data set using Euclidean distance, a subjective pruning of the tree would lead to the recognition of two major clusters at one level, and possibly three if different levels of the tree are considered. This procedure is hardly satisfactory because it is generally biased by the needs and opinions of the researcher as to the "correct" structure of the data.

A more formal, but still heuristic, approach to the problem is to graph the number of clusters implied by a hierarchical tree against the fusion or amalgamation coefficient, which is the numerical value at which various cases merge to form a cluster. The values of the fusion coefficients are shown along the y-axis in the tree diagram. This test, a variant of which was proposed by Thorndike in 1953, is analogous to the "scree test" of factor analysis. A marked "flattening" in this graph suggests that no new information is portrayed by the following mergers

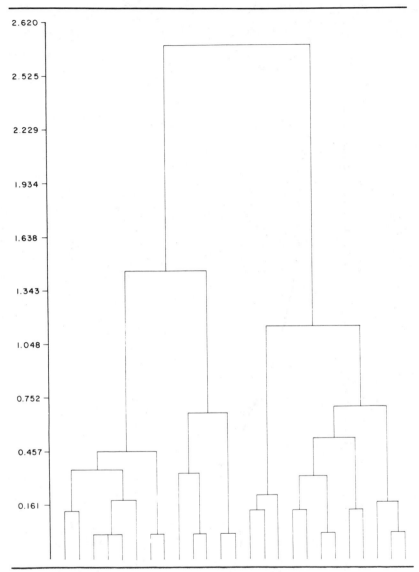

Figure 8: Ward's Method Dendrogram, Full Burial Data Set

of clusters. Figure 9 shows this type of graph for the full burial data set using Ward's method and Euclidean distance. A flattening in the curve begins at the three-cluster solution, and the line is essentially flat at the two-cluster solution, thus implying that three, but most likely two, clusters are present in the data.

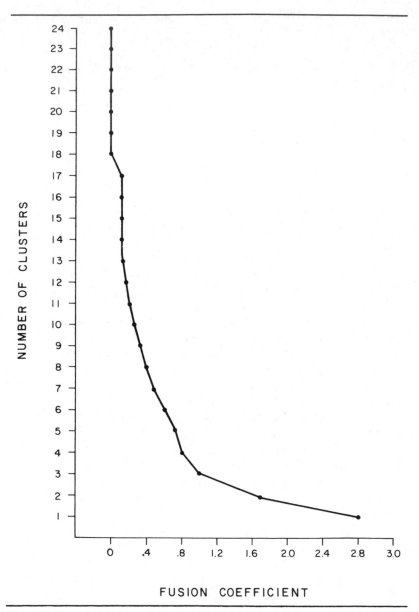

Figure 9: Plot of Number of Clusters Versus Fusion Coefficient, Ward's Method
Solution of Full Burial Data Set

Another subjective procedure that has been made more formal is one that again examines the values of the fusion coefficients to discover a significant "jump" in the value of the coefficient. A jump implies that two relatively dissimilar clusters have been merged; thus the number of clusters prior to the merger is the most probable solution. Shown below are the fusion coefficients associated with the number of clusters ranging from 10 to 1 for the full burial data set.

10 clusters	.312	5 clusters	.729
9 clusters	.333	4 clusters	.733
8 clusters	.354	3 clusters	1.075
7 clusters	.458	2 clusters	1.708
6 clusters	.642	1 cluster	2.872

A jump between the four- and three-cluster solutions can be seen, thus implying that a four-cluster solution is appropriate. One difficulty with this procedure is that many small jumps in the value of the fusion coefficient can be found, and there is really no way to tell through simple visual inspection which of these is the "correct" one.

Mojena (1977) and Mojena and Wishart (1980) have extended this test and have developed a heuristic procedure by which a "significant jump" in the coefficient can be better defined. "Stopping rule #1," as defined by Mojena (1977), states that a group level or optimal partition of a hierarchical clustering solution is selected that satisfies the inequality

$$z_{j+1} > z + ks_z$$

where z is the value of the fusion coefficient, z_j+1 is the value of the coefficient at stage $j + 1$ of the clustering process, k is the standard deviate, and z and s_z are the mean and standard deviation of the fusion coefficients, respectively. If the inequality cannot be satisfied, this suggests that the data have only one cluster.

In practice, the standard deviate can be calculated for each stage in the clustering process, where k is

$$k_j = \left\{ z_{j+1} - z \right\} / s_z$$

The values of the fusion coefficients for the full burial data set as clustered by Ward's method using Euclidean distance were listed above; the values for the standard deviate for 1 to 4 clusters are the following:

	Fusion coefficients	Standard deviates
4 clusters	.458	.472
3 clusters	.974	1.074
2 clusters	1.929	1.707
1 cluster	3.684	2.871

In this case the stopping rule indicates that a three-cluster solution is optimal. Wishart (1982) notes that it is possible to test the statistical significance of the results of this rule with the t-statistic with n-2 degrees of freedom, where n is the number of fusion coefficients. The procedure is to multiply the square root of n − 1 and the value of the standard deviate k. In this case the values are 4.79 (the square root of 23) times .974, which yields 4.67. This value is significant at the .01 level for 22 degrees of freedom. This method, along with a more sophisticated rule, is now implemented in CLUSTAN 2.

The development of formal statistical tests has not been appreciably slowed by the formidable problems of complex multivariate sampling distributions, but few tests have been widely accepted. The most common null hypothesis used in these tests is that the data under study are a random sample from a multivariate normal distribution. If this assumption seems reasonable, Wolfe (1971) has proposed a likelihood ratio test that tests the hypothesis that r, rather that r' groups are present. An alternative hypothesis developed by Lee (1979) is that the data are a random sample of a uniform distribution. Tests based upon this hypothesis use the within-groups sum of squares criterion that appears to be at least a useful starting point in determining the possible differences between clusters. Unfortunately, the test is capable of dealing with only a single variable.

Whatever the procedure chosen, the user must be constantly aware that few of these tests have been studied extensively, and that since most are poorly understood or are heuristics, the results of their use should be treated with considerable caution. Ideally, these rules on how to determine the number of clusters present should be used in conjunction with an appropriate validation procedure (see Chapter 4) because it is possible that the stopping rule may propose a number of clusters that may not be valid as measured by other criteria.

Comparing Clustering Methods

Since different clustering methods can produce different results when applied to the same data, it is important to explore some of the reasons this occurs. We have noted throughout the text that certain methods have inherent biases in them; single linkage tends to find long, chained clusters, whereas Ward's method is biased in favor of tight, hyperspherical clusters. The recognition that different clustering methods will generate markedly different results is much more than an academic curiosity, because these methods are routinely applied to the study of real-world data. Knowing the strengths and weaknesses of different methods prior to an exhaustive analysis of data is preferable to discovering that the results of the analysis are due more to the characteristics of the method itself than any inherent structure of the data.

Most comparisons of clustering methods have been based upon the evaluation of how well different clustering methods recover the structure of data sets with known stucture. Although real-world data with these characteristics have been used in some of these studies, most have used artificial data created primarily through Monte Carlo simulation and sampling. In many cases, the data have been created to mimic real data, such as the simulated MMPI data created by Blashfield and Morey (1980). More frequently, data sets have been created according to the properties of important distributional forms, such as the bivariate normal, multivariate normal, and multivariate gamma distributions. Depending on the goals of the comparison, these data sets have varied in size (the number of cases per cluster), shape of the clusters, number of clusters present, degree of overlap between clusters, presence of outliers, and conditions of coverage (whether or not a classification must be exhaustive). Still other comparisons have been based upon data sets that satisfy the ultrametric inequality, a more stringent condition of the triangle inequality described in Chapter 2 (Milligan and Issac, 1980). Some attention has also been paid to the effects of using different similarity measures.

The results of these studies are difficult to summarize, because each has emphasized different combinations of data structure and methods tested; thus it should not be surprising that contradictory results have been obtained (Milligan, 1981). However, four factors appear to influence greatly the performance of clustering methods:

(1) elements of cluster structure,

(2) the presence of outliers and the degree of coverage required,

(3) the degree of cluster overlap, and

(4) choice of similarity measure.

The most important elements of cluster structure that affect the performance of clustering methods are cluster shape, cluster size (both in terms of the total number of entities per cluster and the relative size differences between clusters), and the number of clusters. We have already shown in a number of circumstances that certain clustering methods are biased toward the discovery of certain types of clusters. Space-dilating methods, such as Ward's method and complete linkage, and the use of the trW criterion for iterative partitioning procedures, all tend to find hyperspherical clusters, and it should be no surprise that those Monte Carlo studies that have constructed clusters of this shape have shown space-dilating methods to provide superior recovery of known cluster structure when compared to space-contracting methods. It is not surprising that these methods usually fail to recover the structure of elongated or oddly shaped clusters. Space-dilating methods have the further tendency to find clusters of nearly equal sizes, and Monte Carlo studies have shown that clusters with relatively few cases may be inappropriately absorbed into larger clusters. Mojena (1977) has suggested that Ward's method, in particular, is adversely affected when the number of groups present in the data increases, but this result has not yet been replicated in other Monte Carlo work. In general, space-contracting methods such as single linkage work well under conditions of cluster structure in which space-dilating methods fail, and what Monte Carlo evidence exists supports the claim that space-contracting methods can indeed provide adequate recovery of known cluster structure if clusters are well-defined and separated.

The presence of outliers and the degree of coverage required of a clustering method have also been identified as important factors in method performance. Total coverage implies a classification that is exhaustive; all cases under consideration must be placed into a group. Monte Carlo studies of this factor have shown that if complete coverage of a classification is required, and the data have relatively few outliers, Ward's method provides superior recovery of known cluster structure (Kuiper and Fisher, 1975; Mojena, 1977). However, Blashfield and Morey (1980), Edelbrock (1979), Edelbrock and McLaughlin (1979), and Milligan (1980) have shown that average linkage clustering provides at least similar cluster recovery to Ward's method if the degree of coverage is decreased. Milligan and Issac (1980), using ultrametric data, have shown that average linkage may in fact do better than Ward's method even when complete coverage is required. In general, it appears that space-dilating methods may be adversely affected by the presence of large numbers of outliers, but this situation is far from clear. It is important to remember that outliers are not simply aberrant cases, but may in fact be representatives of poorly sampled subgroups of cases. Therefore, the obvious solution to this problem, the discard of these cases, should not be the routine solution. Whatever their interpretation, outliers should be identified before cluster analysis is used, and each should be carefully evaluated to determine the reason it is so different from the other cases.

The problem of cluster overlap is similar to that of coverage and the presence of outliers in a sample of data. Cluster overlap is simply the degree to which clusters occupy the same space. Clusters may be well separated, or they may be close to one another. Also, noise points—data points that lie between the boundaries of clusters—may be present. All of these conditions have been shown to have significant effects on the performance of clustering methods. Once again, in conditions of cluster overlap, Ward's method has been shown to outperform most other clustering methods (Bayne et al., 1980), while average linkage tends to do poorly (Bayne et al., 1980; Milligan, 1980). However, all other factors being equal, average linkage provides equivalent coverage to Ward's method when clusters are well separated, and if conditions of coverage are relaxed and overlap is present, this method is again equivalent to the performance of Ward's method (Edelbrock, 1979; Edelbrock and McLaughlin, 1979; Milligan, 1980).

Finally, the choice of similarity measure also has an effect on the performance of clustering methods. Unfortunately, only two measures have been studied: Euclidean distance and the product-moment correlation coefficient. In virtually all of the Monte Carlo studies described above, Ward's method using Euclidean distance and average linkage using the product-moment coefficient were compared in performance. While it seems that the choice of coefficient does in fact make some difference in the resulting solution, these effects seem to be swamped by factors of cluster structure, degree of coverage required, and overlap of clusters. Much more work on other coefficients is necessary before the effects of similarity methods on the performance of clustering methods can be evaluated.

Suggested Reading

In this chapter a number of the various methods that are included under the generic title of "cluster analysis" have been described. This chapter does not by any means present all clustering methods, nor does it comprehensively discuss all that is known about the methods that are discussed. For novices who wish to read other introductions to the various clustering methods, Bailey (1975), Everitt (1980), and Lorr (1983) are recommended. All three are quite readable, but vary somewhat in their orientation. For more sophisticated readers, the review by Cormack (1971), despite being dated, is a must, as is Everitt's (1979) summary of unresolved problems in this literature. In addition, there are five books that contain a great deal of detailed information about various clustering methods and their performance: Anderberg (1973), Clifford and Stephenson (1975), Hartigan (1975), Mezzich and Solomon (1980), and Sneath and Sokal (1973).

4. VALIDATION TECHNIQUES

This chapter discusses five techniques for validating a cluster analysis solution: (1) the cophenetic correlation, (2) significance tests on variables used to create clusters, (3) replication, (4) significance tests on independent variables, and (5) Monte Carlo procedures.

Cophenetic Correlation

The cophenetic correlation was first proposed by Sokal and Rohlf (1962) and is the major validation measure advocated by the numerical taxonomists (Sneath and Sokal, 1973). This measure is appropriate only when a hierarchical agglomerative method of clustering is used. The cophenetic correlation is used to determine how well the tree or dendrogram resulting from a hierarchical method actually represents the pattern of similarities/dissimilarities among the entities.

The hierarchical tree in Figure 3 shows the single linkage solution using Jaccard's coefficient to the six-entity burial data. Simply by examining this tree, one can infer the similarities between any pair of entities. For instance, entities TFE (teenage, female, elite) and AFE (adult, female, elite) are fairly similar since they merged at a relatively "high" branch in the tree. On the other hand, entities CFE and TFE are relatively dissimilar since they are not merged into a common cluster until the last clustering step (i.e., they are merged at the base of the tree).

By using the tree shown in Figure 3, it is possible to create an implied similarity matrix that shows the similarities between all pairs of entities as sugested by this hierarchical solution:

	CMN	CFE	TMN	TFE	AME	AFE
CMN	–	.250	.333	.333	.333	.333
CFE		–	.250	.250	.250	.250
TMN			–	.500	.500	.500
TFE				–	.500	.750
AME					–	.500
AFE						–

Each value represents the similarity value at which the respective pair of entities was merged into a common cluster. An important point to note regarding this similarity matrix is that there are at most only $N - 1$ (i.e., five) unique values in this matrix since hierarchical agglomerative methods always require $N - 1$ merger steps. In contrast, the original similarity matrix contains $N(N - 1)/2$ unique values, excluding ties. The original similarity matrix is

	CMN	CFE	TMN	TFE	AME	AFE
CMN	–	.000	.250	.250	.333	.200
CFE		–	.000	.250	.143	.200
TMN			–	.200	.500	.167
TFE				–	.500	.750
AME					–	.429
AFE						–

The cophenetic correlation is the correlation between the values in the original similarity matrix and the values in the implied similarity matrix. Thus the cophenetic correlation of the single linkage solution as shown in Figure 3 is $C = 0.810$.

Despite its rather frequent use, the cophenetic correlation does have distinct problems. First, the use of the product-moment correlation assumes normal distributions of the values in the two matrices being correlated. This assumption is generally violated for the values in the implied similarity matrix since the clustering method used largely determines the distribution of the similarity values in this matrix. Thus the use of the correlation coefficient is not an optimal estimator of the degree of similarity between the values in the two matrices. Second, since the number of unique values in the implied similarity matrix is much smaller than the number of unique values in the original similarity matrix, the amount of information contained in the two matrices is quite different. Holgersson (1978) performed a Monte Carlo study to analyze the characteristics of the cophenetic correlation and found it generally to be a misleading indicator of the quality of the cluster solution.

Significance Tests on Variables
Used to Create Clusters

Another procedure that has been used frequently in applied research involving cluster analysis is to perform a multivariate analysis of variance (MANOVA) of the variables used to generate the solution in order to test for the significance of the clusters.[3] In contrast to the use of the cophenetic correlation that attempts to analyze the accuracy of the hierarchical tree, the performance of standard significance tests is concerned with the quality of the cluster solution as a partition of the data set. Thus, the MANOVA technique can be used on solutions from any clustering technique that creates partitions (e.g., iterative partitioning methods, hierarchical methods, factor analysis variants).

Intuitively, the use of MANOVA to perform significance tests on the clusters is plausible. Moreover, it becomes an appealing procedure because the results are invariably highly significant, thus the procedure looks impressive when the cluster solution is written up for a journal article. For instance, the Filsinger et al. (1979) study of religious individuals as discussed in Chapter 1 found significant differences among the clusters when a discriminant analysis was performed on the variables used in creating the clusters. In fact, the discriminant analysis correctly classified 96 percent of the subjects. These results certainly suggest that the Filsinger et al. cluster solution is a good descriptive representation of types of religious individuals. However, *the use of discriminant analysis (or MANOVA or multiple ANOVAs) in this fashion is inappropriate statistically.*

To understand this, consider the following example. Suppose that a group of researchers performed routine IQ tests on a set of randomly selected children from one grade throughout an entire school system, and suppose further that there are no clusters of children in this data set.

When the researchers plot the data along the dimension of IQ scores, they find a normal distribution with a mean of 100—exactly what would have been predicted from normative data on this variable. Nonetheless, suppose they also decide to perform a cluster analysis on these data despite the unimodal distribution along the IQ variables. The resulting cluster solution splits the sample into two groups: children with IQ scores above 100 and children with IQ scores of 100 or less. If the researchers then perform an analysis of variance to compare the two groups in terms of their IQ scores, the resulting F test will be highly significant! This "highly significant" result will occur despite the fact that no clusters exist in the data. Cluster analysis methods, by definition, will separate entities into clusters that have virtually no overlap along the variables being used to create the clusters. Significance tests for differences among the clusters along these variables should always be positive. Since these tests are positive, regardless of whether clusters exist in the data or not, the performance of these tests is useless at best and misleading at worst.

Replication

The first two validation techniques described in this chapter are frequently used, but both have serious problems. Methodologists in the area of cluster analysis do not consider either of them to be a useful validation technique (Hartigan, 1975a).

The third technique involves the estimation of the degree of replicability of a cluster solution across a series of data sets. If a cluster solution is repeatedly discovered across different samples from the same general population, it is plausible to conclude that this solution has some generality. A cluster solution that is not stable is unlikely to have general utility. This technique was exemplified in Chapter 1 in the review of the Goldstein and Linden (1969) study of alcoholics in which they split their sample into two parts and performed the same method of cluster analysis on both parts. They reported that the same four clusters appeared in the two solutions.

The replication technique, in effect, is a check for the internal consistency of a solution. To show that the same clusters appear across different subsets when the same clustering method is used is *not* strong evidence for the validity of a solution. In other words, the failure of a cluster solution to replicate is reason for rejecting the solution, but a successful replication does not guarantee the validity of the solution.

Significance Tests on External Variables

The procedures included in this category are probably among the better ways to validate a clustering solution, but, unfortunately, this approach has been little used despite its potential importance. Basically, the procedure is to perform significance tests that compare the clusters on variables *not* used to generate the cluster solution. This technique—used in the study of religious individuals by Filsinger et al. (1979), who contrasted their clusters along seven demographic variables that were not used in forming the clusters (see Chapter 1)—found significant differences along four of these seven variables.

An interesting study that employed an even more elaborate external validation test of a cluster solution was performed by Finney and Moos (1979). These investigators, like Goldstein and Linden (1969) in the study reviewed in Chapter 1, wanted to determine if subtypes of alcoholism could be defined. They analyzed questionnaire data on 429 alcoholic patients and found eight clusters. On these same patients, six month follow-up data were available along five variables: (1) self-reported alcohol consumption, (2) abstinence, (3) physical impairment, (4) rehabilitation, and (5) occupational functioning. Finney and Moos found that the eight clusters were different on these five variables as was demonstrated by significant F statistics using one-way ANOVAs. Also, the researchers found a significant association between the type of treatment program in which the patient was enrolled and cluster membership. However, there was no type X treatment interaction along any of the five outcome measures.

The power of external validation is that it directly tests the generality of a cluster solution against relevant criteria. One reason this approach to validation is not used frequently in cluster analysis research is that the methodological design necessary to collect relevant criterion data is usually expensive. Another likely reason is that in many cases it is difficult to define a set of relevant external criteria because the avowed use of cluster analysis in this context may be essentially exploratory or, in some instances, because the necessary theory surrounding the classification process has not yet been refined sufficiently to determine what is truly relevant to the intended classification. However, the value of a cluster solution that has successfully passed an external validation is much greater than a solution that has not.

Monte Carlo Procedures

The last approach to validation has had relatively little use and is somewhat complicated to explain. Basically, this approach is to use

Monte Carlo procedures, using random number generators, to create a data set with general characteristics matching the overall characteristics of the original data but containing no clusters. The same clustering methods are used on both the real data and the artificial data, and the resulting solutions are compared by appropriate methods. An example, using the MMPI data, of this process is perhaps the best way to illustrate this approach.

Step 1: Creation of the Monte Carlo data set. Using random number generators, an artificial data set is created. This data set has no clusters but has the same overall characteristics as the original data set. To accomplish this, we calculated the grand means, standard deviations, and variable-by-variable correlation matrix for the original 90-patient MMPI data set. Next, we wrote a brief FORTRAN program to create the Monte Carlo data set that utilizes a random number generator subroutine from the IMSL collection of programs. This subroutine generates data points that are sampled from a multivariate normal distribution with a specified mean vector and covariance matrix. This step may seem somewhat formidable to a user, but, in fact, the program is relatively easy to write and only required 36 lines of FORTRAN. The output of this FORTRAN program was a Monte Carlo data set that also had 90 hypothetical patients but had no clusters in the data.

Step 2: Performing the same method of cluster analysis on both data sets. In order to compare the results of a cluster analysis on the data sets, a k-means iterative partitioning method was performed on each data set using BMDPKM. The program starts with an internally generated starting partition and iteratively uses the k-means method described in Chapter 3 to form a specified number of clusters. Because we knew that the original data consisted of three groups, we decided to look at only a three-cluster solution.

The means found in the Monte Carlo data are quite different from means of the actual groups in the original data. The reader will also note that the means of these groups can be roughly ordered along an elevation continuum. That is, one cluster contains generally elevated profiles, another contains moderately elevated profiles, and the means for the third cluster are relatively low. Our experience with using cluster analysis on Monte Carlo data suggests that many clustering methods form clusters from random data that are organized along an elevation continuum.

Step 3: Comparison of the cluster solution. The last step is to compare the output statistics of the cluster solutions obtained from the real and artificial data sets. In this case, we used the F-ratio validation measure of the BMDPKM program. One indicator is the F-ratio values calculated from performing one-way ANOVAs among the clusters on all 13 variables. These F-ratio values are shown below.

L	9.4	Mf	1.5
F	69.7	Pa	63.7
K	10.6	Pt	26.4
Hs	47.7	Sc	59.3
D	27.6	Ma	27.7
Hy	21.1	Si	27.9
Pd	38.5		

Note that most of these values are quite large; in fact, with the exception of the value for the Mf scale, the F ratios range from 9.4 to 69.7. If significance tests were performed using these 13 variables, 12 would appear to be significant. However, as discussed above the use of significance tests in this manner is inappropriate.

The next set of values shown below are the corresponding F-ratios for the three-cluster solution to the Monte Carlo data. Since there are actually no clusters in the Monte Carlo data, these values are one-point estimates of the null values for these F-ratios. Generally, the values of these F-ratios are about as large or larger than the F-ratios of the original data. In fact, these F-ratios range in value from 11.9 to 77.4 (again excluding the Mf scale).

L	13.7	Mf	0.1
F	22.6	Pa	36.4
K	52.4	Pt	77.4
Hs	18.8	Sc	67.4
D	55.7	Ma	19.8
Hy	11.9	Si	31.2
Pd	14.9		

What does this comparison suggest? The F-ratio calculated in the BMDPKM program is designed to give the user some indication of cluster homogeneity. When one analyzes the absolute values of the first set of F-ratios, these values seem reasonably large and appear to suggest that the clusters have some degree of homogeneity. However, the F-ratios for the no-cluster data are just as large, suggesting in effect that the first set of F-ratios are not sufficiently large that a user could reject the null hypothesis of no clusters.

The graphical output from the BMDPKM program can be used to visually portray the pattern of results. Figure 10 shows a scatterplot for the three clusters as represented in a two-dimensional principal compo-

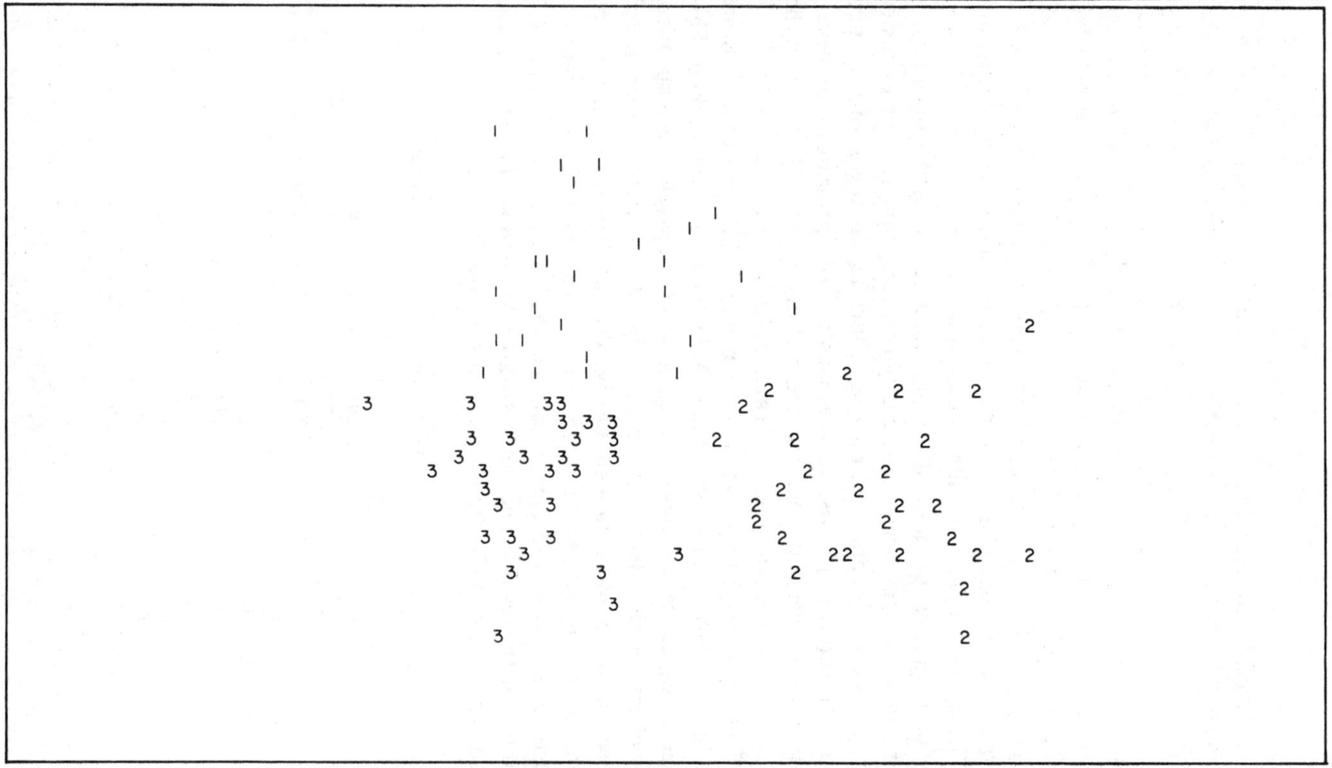

Figure 10: Scatterplot of Three-Cluster Solution, Original MMPI Data

nents space. In this plot, the three clusters can be seen relatively clearly. However, when the clusters from the Monte Carlo data are also plotted (Figure 11), three "clusters" appear that have no overlap, but that are not quite as dense as the actual clusters shown in Figure 10. Note that in both scatterplots there are no obvious boundaries between clusters. Instead, in both solutions, the graphical output suggests that the clusters could simply be an arbitrary partition of the total data. Thus, the comparison of the graphical output from the original data with the output on the Monte Carlo data makes it clear that the user would have difficulty rejecting the null hypothesis of no clusters.

The important point is that from examination of the output of a computer program, one might easily conclude that the three-cluster solution was valid, and that relatively discrete, homogeneous clusters had been formed. The use of the Monte Carlo procedure, however, provides a comparative basis for interpreting the output statistics of the clustering programs in a more formal manner.

To give the reader a more positive example of the use of the Monte Carlo procedure, another 90-patient MMPI data set was studied. This data set was chosen so that the three groups (i.e., psychotics, neurotics, and character disorders) were very tightly defined, and the existence of three clusters in these data should be obvious. Again, the three steps were carried out: (1) forming a Monte Carlo data set, (2) performing a cluster analysis on both the original and the Monte Carlo data, and (3) comparing the results. The same BMDPKM method of clustering was used. The resulting F-ratio output statistics are shown below.

	Actual data	Monte Carlo data
L	55.1	19.1
F	895.2	91.4
K	70.2	37.6
Hs	250.9	39.4
D	115.1	37.4
Hy	151.4	25.1
Pd	414.3	28.5
Mf	4.1	3.9
Pa	497.5	75.9
Pt	129.5	72.1
Sc	365.0	91.8
Ma	370.9	30.0
Si	243.7	59.4

Note how much larger the F-ratios for the original data are than for the Monte Carlo data. Virtually all F-ratios are three-digit numbers for the

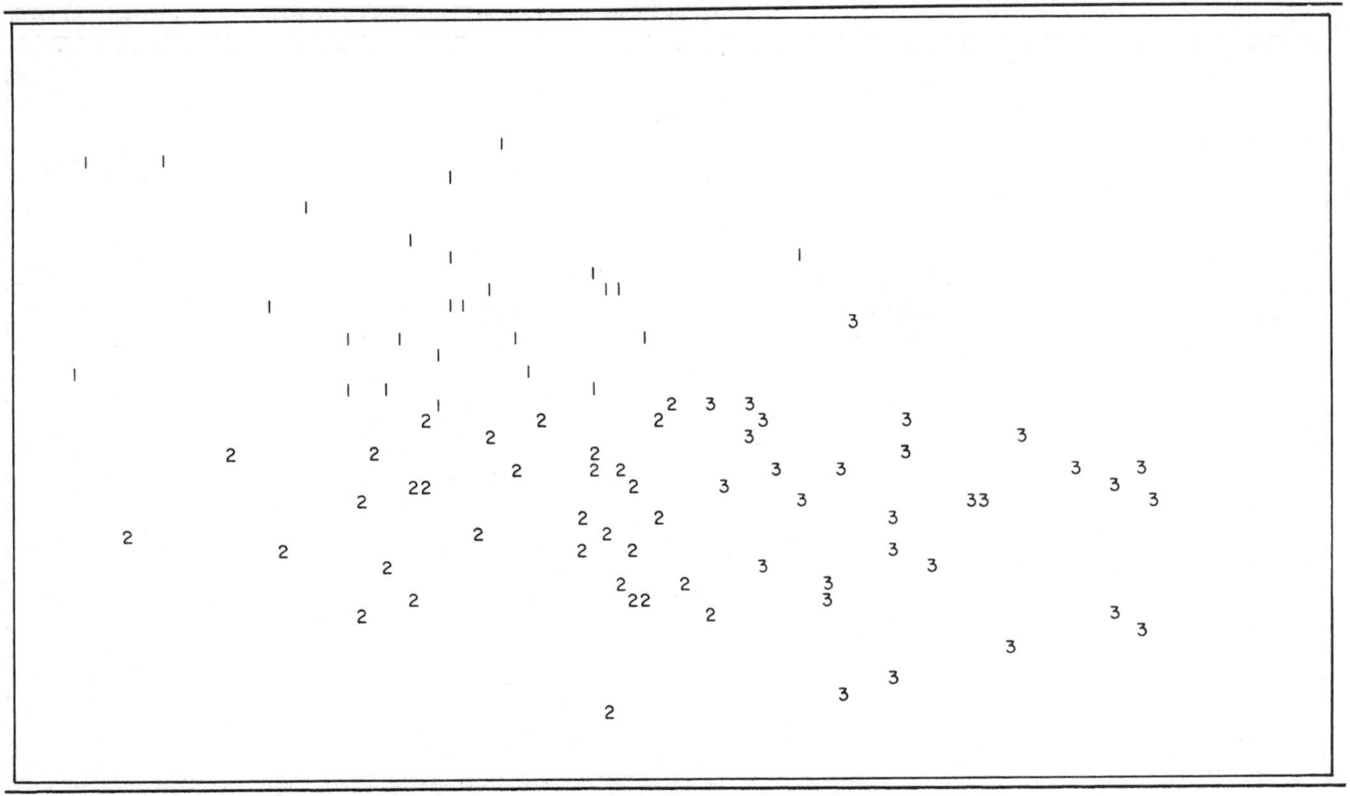

Figure 11: Scatterplot of Three-Cluster Solution, Monte Carlo MMPI Data

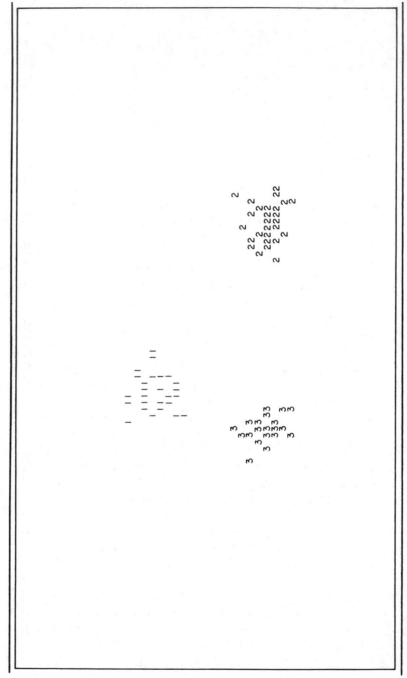

Figure 12: Scatterplot of Three-Cluster Solution, Tightly Clustered MMPI Data

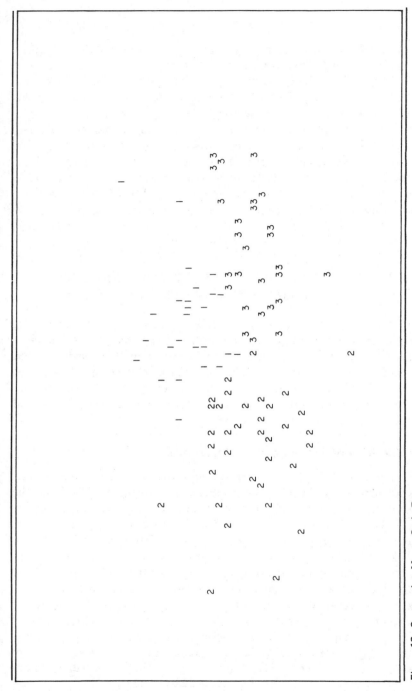

Figure 13: Scatterplot, Monte Carlo Data

73

actual data and would seem very large values by any standards. Figures 12 and 13 show the comparative cluster scatterplots for the original and the Monte Carlo data, respectively. Notice that with the original data, the clusters are very tight, and there exist clear boundaries among the clusters. This pattern is not noted for the Monte Carlo data.

Although most validation procedures are not well understood, and while their use in applied research should be handled cautiously, the use of some type of validation procedure is necessary in any cluster analysis study. Readers interested in pursuing the topic of cluster validation are encouraged to read Dubes and Jain (1980), Rohlf (1974), Skinner and Blashfield (1982), and Chambers and Kleiner (1982).

5. CLUSTER ANALYSIS SOFTWARE AND THE LITERATURE ON CLUSTERING

Clustering software can be placed into four major categories: (1) collections of subroutines and algorithms, (2) general statistical packages that contain clustering methods, (3) cluster analysis packages, and (4) simple programs that perform one type of clustering (Blashfield et al., 1982). Since a comprehensive review of clustering software is beyond the scope of this text, we shall focus upon only those programs and packages that are widely available.

Collections of Subroutines and Algorithms

Three major collections of software are available today in this category: books by Anderberg (1973) and Hartigan (1975), and the routines in the International Mathematical and Statistical Library (IMSL, 1980). Although much of this software is fairly sophisticated, the user must supply all job control language of the computing system to link and subsequently run the routines. Thus, to borrow current computer jargon, this software is not very "user friendly." The user must be very familiar with local job control language as well as FORTRAN, the language used to develop these routines, simply to be able to get them running. In general, the level of user support for these routines is low; Hartigan's algorithms are described in a separate user's manual (Dallal, 1975), whereas Anderberg's algorithms are only supported in his book. While the IMSL clustering algorithms are imbedded within the documentation of the entire collection of IMSL subroutines, the documentation does not necessarily make them any easier to use. Despite the breadth of methods available and some interesting options, algorithms in this category are not recommended for use by the novice unless extensive guidance is available.

Statistical Packages Containing Clustering Software

Perhaps the most convenient cluster analysis software available for general use is that contained within popular packages of statistical programs such as BMDP (Dixon, 1983), SAS (SAS Institute, 1982), and SPSS (SPSS, 1984). The philosophy of these packages is well known; they provide nonprogrammers with relatively easy access to sophisticated statistical methods for a wide variety of research problems. The packages provide an umbrella of support for the user in that they use a consistent control language that communicates the needs of the user to the computing system with a minimum of effort. These packages also contain a full range of data screening and manipulation methods that help to make complex analyses simple and feasible. If the package contains the method of interest to the user, the advantages of using existing statistical packages are substantial.

With the exception of BMDP, the range of clustering options contained in most statistical packages has been severely limited. For instance, early releases of SAS contained only one clustering method, and SPSS had none. However, this state of affairs has changed dramatically. BMDP has developed four procedures devoted to cluster analysis: (1) a collection of single, complete, and average linkage algorithms to cluster variables; (2) average linkage (centroid sorting), single linkage, and k-nearest neighbor methods to cluster cases; (3) a block clustering method (Hartigan, 1975a) to simultaneously cluster cases and variables; and (4) an iterative k-means method that forms partitions among the cases. (The last procedure, BMDPKM, was used in the example of the Monte Carlo replication technique in Chapter 4). The BMDP procedures are well annotated, have clear output and are relatively easy to use. The most serious limitations of this package are the limited range of hierarchical agglomerative methods for clustering cases, and the choice of only four similarity measures (Euclidean distance, the Minkowski metric, a chi-square measure, and the phi coefficient).

The second statistical package, SAS, until recently contained one method of cluster analysis—complete linkage. However, the most recent release of this package, SAS 1982, includes substantial additions, although, curiously, the package no longer includes the complete linkage option. The package (within a procedure called CLUSTER) now contains centroid, Ward's, and average linkage hierarchical agglomerative methods. Euclidean distance is still the only similarity measure offered. In procedure FASTCLUS, a k-means method (Anderberg's centroid sorting method) has been added, and finally, a factor analysis-type variable clustering method has been included (procedure VARCLUS). The diagnostics of the package have been expanded and are similar to those offered by CLUSTAN. Of considerable interest is the inclusion of a new stopping procedure for the determination of the number of clusters — the cubic clustering criterion. This procedure has been included in the latest release of the package, but the authors of SAS have not published any studies that demonstrate the validity or the utility of this procedure for applied research.

SPSS currently contains no method of cluster analysis. However, there is a new procedure called CLUSTER (Bajaj, 1979) that is being considered for possible inclusion in the SPSS collection. This new procedure contains 27 similarity measures, most of which are association coefficients. Seven hierarchical agglomerative methods—including single linkage, complete linkage, average linkage, and Ward's method—can be used.

Cluster Analysis Packages

For the serious user of cluster analysis, cluster analysis packages represent the ultimate of flexibility and user convenience. These packages combine the advantages of general statistical packages, such as an integrated control language and data screening and manipulation procedures, with features of interest to users of cluster analysis, such as a diversity of clustering methods, special diagnostic features, and enhanced graphics. Of the greatest importance is that many of the packages contain hard-to-find or unique clustering methods or analytical procedures that are appropriate for special problems or data structures.

The most popular of the packages devoted to cluster analysis is CLUSTAN. The newest release of CLUSTAN (version 2.1; Wishart, 1982) contains eleven procedures that invoke all of the families of clustering methods defined in Chapter 3 with the exception of factor analysis variants. These procedures are

HIERARCHY—eight hierarchical agglomerative methods

CENTROID —centroid hierarchical method

RELOCATE —iterative k-means method

MODE   —mode analysis

DENSITY   —an improved mode analysis method
DIVIDE   —monothetic divisive method

KDEND —graph theoretic method of Jardine and Sibson

DNDRITE —minimum spanning tree method

EUCLID —iterative method using nonlinear programming

NORMIX —method designed to decompose multivariate normal-mixtures

INVARIANT —iterative method designed to optimize multivariate indicators of cluster homogeneity

Among the other features of CLUSTAN are cluster diagnostic and validation aids, including procedures RULES and COMPARE, that implement the stopping rules of Mojena (1977) and the cophenetic correlation coefficient of Mojena and Wishart (1980). A total of 38 similarity measures are contained in procedure CORREL, and the package has a utility procedure that permits the user to define any type of similarity coefficient (DEFINE). Other important utilities are those that prepare a number of cluster diagnostics or that produce a wide variety of graphical output.

CLUSTAN is the most versatile of the available clustering packages. The manual for CLUSTAN is reasonably well written, but it does require moderate sophistication in both cluster analysis and computer software. Serious users of cluster analysis will find this package very useful, but the user should be aware that this package, despite its versatility, does not exhaust options available in other software.

There are three other packages that are devoted to cluster analysis: BCTRY (Tryon and Bailey, 1970), CLUS (Friedman and Rubin, 1967), and NTSYS (Rohlf et al., 1974). Of these three, NTSYS is the most important because it incorporates the methods and the ideas discussed in the frequently cited book on cluster analysis and numerical taxonomy: Sneath and Sokal (1973). NTSYS contains a number of multivariate statistical procedures in addition to cluster analysis, including multidimensional scaling and factor analysis. The BCTRY package is based on the book by Tryon and Bailey (1970) and includes a series of clustering methods that reflect Tryon's approach to factor analysis. The final package, CLUS, is rarely used currently, and interested users can find a modern version of this program in the newest release of CLUSTAN.

Simple Cluster Analysis Programs

Simple cluster analysis programs are just that—simple. These are programs written primarily in FORTRAN, and they implement one or two clustering algorithms. In some ways they strongly resemble the subroutines of the first category defined above, in that they require the user to be fully competent in the job control language of the computing system as well as the language in which the program is written. In general, these programs have no or few aids for checking programming errors, are poorly documented, and provide limited output information. These programs are important, however, because they have often been used within particular scientific areas, or they have been used to form the basis for the algorithms presented in major packages such as SAS, IMSL, and OSIRIS. Some of the more popular of these simple programs are HGROUP, a method that implements single and complete linkage as discussed in the influential article by Johnson (1967); and ISODATA, a flexible iterative partitioning method that has been used extensively in engineering (Hall and Khanna, 1977).

The Literature on Cluster Analysis

Although classification is a fundamental step in the process of doing science, different sciences have different problems demanding solution, and varying levels of control over the phenomena that structure their domains of inquiry. Therefore, it should not be surprising that cluster analysis, a method advertised as an "objective" means of classification, has taken many forms and been defined in many, sometimes contradictory, ways. It is also natural that the literature on cluster analysis should be found in a variety of journals, ranging from electrical engineering to biology to library science to psychiatry. A recognition of the diversity of the disciplines contributing to the literature of cluster analysis, as well as an appreciation of the variety of methods lumped under the term "cluster analysis," is necessary for the informed and consistent use of the method in any field of research.

In Chapter 1 we described the reasons for the explosion of interest in cluster analysis. Concurrent with the development of new clustering methods and algorithms was a rapid growth in the number of articles concerned with clustering in an expanding number of scientific fields. While the rapid growth of the literature was confined somewhat to the biological sciences in the 1960s, by the late 1960s and early 1970s the method had spread to virtually all fields of scientific endeavor. In 1973, for example, the 292 articles that cited at least one major work on cluster analysis or that had used the terms "cluster analysis" or "numerical taxonomy" in their title were found in 162 journals, including *Acta Psychologica, American Antiquity, Computer Journal, Journal of Biochemistry, Quarterly Journal of Medicine, Journal of Marketing Research, Systematic Zoology,* and *Journal of Ecology* (Blashfield and

Aldenderfer, 1978b). The topics studied ranged from analyses of the penile morphology of mummified New Guinea rodents to the study of voting habits of U.S. senators to an analysis of behavioral latencies of frozen cockroaches during thawing to a study of the geographical distribution of species of lichen in Saskatchewan.

The effects of this literature explosion in the development and use of cluster analysis have been profound, and, unfortunately, some of the most profound effects have been negative. The rapid growth of the literature on cluster analysis has resulted in the formation of cliques of users, and an inevitable outgrowth of clique formation is the creation of jargon that is exclusive to that clique (Blashfield and Aldenderfer, 1978b; Blashfield, 1980).

A good example of the formation of jargon among social science users is illustrated with the diverse terminology of Ward's method. At least four different names for this method are known in the literature, and these do not include the term "Ward's method." These alternative forms are "minimum variance method," "error sum of squares method," "hierarchical grouping to minimize trW," and "HGROUP." The former two phrases simply refer to the criterion that Ward's method seeks to optimize, whereas the third term is based upon the fact that the error sum of squares is simply a monotonic transformation of the trace of W, the within-groups covariance matrix. Finally, the term "HGROUP" has been used extensively because it is the name of a popular computer program that implements Ward's method (Veldman, 1967).

The problem with the development of jargon, of course, is that it impedes interdisciplinary communication, hinders the effective comparison of both the methodology and the results of cluster analyses across different sciences, leads to redundancy of effort (the reinvention of an algorithm in many sciences), and, finally, makes it difficult for new users of the technique to understand fully the methods they choose to employ (Blashfield and Aldenderfer, 1978b). For instance, the authors of one study in the social sciences (Rogers and Linden, 1973) compared three different clustering methods using the same data. They referred to these methods as "hierarchical grouping," "hierarchical clustering or HCS," and "cluster analysis." None of these terms is a common referent to any clustering method. A detailed analysis of their description of how each method works revealed that the methods under analysis were Ward's method, either single or complete linkage, and Lorr's clumping method (Lorr and Radhakrishnan, 1967). A new user of cluster anlaysis would be bewildered by these terms, and would be unable to relate them effectively to any other descriptions of clustering methods. Sophisticated users would certainly be hard-pressed to compare this research to any similar work with which they may be aware. While this example may be extreme, the problem of jargon is widespread.

In recent years, however, it appears that the dramatic growth of cluster analysis has slowed somewhat in terms of both numbers of publications and disciplines to which the method has been introduced. It now seems clear that many disciplines, such as psychology and sociology, are entering a consolidation phase concerning the use of cluster analysis. This phase of the use of clustering is already well established in the biological sciences and in some areas of statistics and engineering, but it must be stressed that not all social sciences have reached this phase.

The consolidation phase of the cluster analysis literature is marked by the gradual reduction of expository articles on the virtues of cluster analysis and a slow but steady increase in those articles that compare the use of different clustering methods in controlled settings. Although articles that are primarily concerned with applications are common, more studies are appearing that are directed toward the discovery of practical measures for the validation of the results obtained from the use of cluster analysis. Consolidation is also marked by serious attempts by statisticians to develop meaningful statistical theories for cluster analysis methods.

Guide to Reporting Cluster Analysis Studies

The goal of this book has been to introduce potential users to the technique of cluster analysis and acquaint them with the great diversity of families, literature, software, and terminology that surround the method. We hope that, after reading this book, users will be better able to make informed decisions about the methods and approaches most suitable to their classificatory needs. We have offered no cookbook recipes for the successful use of clustering, but instead have pointed out those problems of which every user of cluster analysis should be aware and have indicated sources to help with their resolution.

We would, however, like to offer guidelines for the researcher when reporting his or her research to the professional community. While these guidelines may not improve the quality of scientific research, they make it possible to compare the results of clustering studies, which may lead to practical and methodological improvements in the technique.

1. An unambiguous description of the clustering method should be provided. This prescription is clearly directed toward reducing the amount of jargon in the literature. Certainly one standard that has emerged is that contained in Sneath and Sokal (1973); we have followed their terminology in this book and recommend it to others. The name of the method should be accompanied by a relevant citation.

2. *The choice of similarity measure [or statistical criterion if an iterative method is used] should be clearly stated.* As shown in Chapters 2 and 3, the choice of similarity measure can have a profound effect on the resulting cluster analysis solution. If the choice of this measure is omitted from a report, readers are unable to determine if the results obtained from the use of the clustering method are affected by this choice.

3. *The computer program used should be stated.* Blashfield (1977) has shown that different computer programs, while ostensibly performing the same clustering method with identical similarity measures, came up with very different results. In this case, the formulae for the calculation of Euclidean distance differed substantially; while each was correct, only one package did not take the square root of the expression. Unfortunately, each package used the term "Euclidean distance" to describe the similarity measure. Such a seemingly trivial difference can be of great consequence if replication of the results of the study is attempted.

4. *The procedures used to determine the number of clusters should be explained.* Again, this guideline is important should independent investigators attempt to replicate the study. Also, it should be obvious that a simple statement such as, "The ten-cluster solution was chosen for analysis," should not be accepted as adequate unless a complete discussion of the reasons for this choice are presented.

5. *Adequate evidence of the validity of the cluster analysis solution should be presented.* This is perhaps the fundamental step in the use of cluster analysis, and yet it is the one that has been ignored most by both users of the method and consumers of the reports. Different clustering methods can and do provide different results when applied to the same data, and unless researchers can provide evidence of the validity of the results of their analysis that are independent of the method, those results should be treated with skepticism.

APPENDIX
Example Data Sets (Burial Data)

1	C	M	N	1	0	0	1	0	0	0	0
2	C	M	N	0	0	0	1	0	0	0	0
3	C	M	E	1	0	0	1	0	0	1	1
4	C	F	N	1	0	1	0	0	0	0	0
5	C	F	E	0	0	1	0	0	0	1	0
6	C	F	E	1	0	1	0	0	0	1	0
7	T	M	N	1	1	0	1	0	0	0	0
8	T	M	N	0	1	0	1	1	0	0	0
9	T	M	N	1	0	0	1	1	0	0	0
10	T	M	N	1	1	0	1	1	0	0	0
11	T	M	E	1	1	0	1	1	0	1	1
12	T	F	N	0	0	0	0	1	0	0	0
13	T	F	N	1	0	0	0	1	0	0	0
14	T	F	E	1	0	0	0	1	0	1	0
15	A	M	N	1	1	0	1	1	0	0	0
16	A	M	N	0	1	0	1	1	0	0	0
17	A	M	N	1	1	0	1	0	0	0	0
18	A	M	E	1	1	0	1	1	0	1	1
19	A	M	E	1	0	0	1	0	0	1	0
20	A	F	N	0	0	0	0	0	1	0	0
21	A	F	N	1	0	0	0	0	1	0	0
22	A	F	N	0	0	0	0	1	1	0	0
23	A	F	N	1	0	0	0	0	0	0	0
24	A	F	E	1	0	0	0	1	1	1	0
25	A	F	E	1	0	0	0	1	1	1	1

KEY: C = child; T = adolescent; A = adult
M = male; F = female
N = nonelite; E = elite
1 = present; 0 = absent

NOTES

1. As will be shown in Chapter 4, this "validation procedure" does not provide any evidence for the validity of the clusters.

2. Eigenvalues are often used in standard factor analysis to give some indication of how important the factors are and to help resolve how many factors exist in the data.

3. For the purposes of this discussion, performing a MANOVA will be considered equivalent to performing a series of one-way analyses of variance on each variable used to create the clusters or to performing a discriminant analysis.

REFERENCES

ANDERBERG, M. (1973) Cluster Analysis for Applications. New York: Academic Press.
BAILEY, K. (1975) "Cluster Analysis," in D. Heise (ed.) Sociological Methodology. San Francisco: Jossey-Bass.
BAJAJ, S. R. (1979) "A preliminary version of subprogram CLUSTER." Applications Division, Northwestern University. (unpublished)
BAYNE, R., J. BEAUCHAMP, C. BEGOVICH, and V. KANE (1980) "Monte Carlo comparisons of selected clustering procedures." Pattern Recognition 12: 51-62.
BLASHFIELD, R. K. (1980) "The growth of cluster analysis: Tryon, Ward, and Johnson." Multivariate Behavioral Research 15: 439-458.
——— (1977) "On the equivalence of four software programs for performing hierarchical cluster analysis." Psychometrika 42: 429-431.
——— (1976) "Mixture model tests of cluster analysis: accuracy of four agglomerative hierarchical methods." Psychological Bulletin 83: 377-388.
——— and M. ALDENDERFER (1978a) "Computer programs for performing iterative partitioning cluster analysis." Applied Psychological Measurement 2: 533-541.
——— (1978b) "The literature on cluster analysis." Multivariate Behavioral Research 13: 271-295.
——— and L. MOREY (1982) "Cluster analysis software," pp. 245-266 in P. Krishnaiah and L. Kanal (eds.) Handbook of Statistics, vol. 2. Amsterdam: North-Holland.
BLASHFIELD, R. and L. MOREY (1980) "A comparison of four clustering methods using MMPI Monte Carlo data." Applied Psychological Measurement 4(1): 57-64.
BONNER, R. E. (1964) "On some clustering techniques." I.B.M. Journal of Research and Development 8: 22-32.
BURTON, M. L. and A. K. ROMNEY (1975) "A multidimensional representation of role terms." American Ethnologist 2: 397-408.
CARMICHAEL, J. W. and P.H.A. SNEATH (1969) "Taxometric maps." Systematic Zoology 18: 267-276.
CLIFFORD, H. and W. STEPHENSON (1975) An Introduction to Numerical Taxonomy. New York: Academic Press.
COLE, A. J. and D. WISHART (1970) "An improved algorithm for the Jardine-Sibson method of generating overlapping clusters." Computer Journal 13: 156-163.
CORMACK, R. (1971) "A review of classification." Journal of the Royal Statistical Society (Series A) 134: 321-367.
CRONBACH, L. and G. GLESER (1953) "Assessing similarity between profiles." Psychological Bulletin 50: 456-473.
CZEKANOWSKI, J. (1911) "Objectiv kriterien in der ethnologie." Korrespondenz-blatt der Deutschen Gesellschaft für Anthropologie, Ethnologie, und Urgeschichte 42: 1-5.
DALLAL, G. E. (1975) "A users' guide to J. A. Hartigan's clustering algorithms." Yale University. (unpublished)
DeJONG, G., J. FAULKNER, and R. WARLAND (1976) "Dimensions of religiosity reconsidered: evidence from a cross-cultural study." Social Forces 54: 866-889.
DIXON, W. (1983) BMDP Statistical Software. Berkeley: University of California Press.
DRIVER, H. E. (1965) "Survey of numerical classification in anthropology," pp. 304-344 in D. Hymes (ed.) The Use of Computers in Anthropology. The Hague: Mouton.

DUBES, R. and A. JAIN (1980) "Clustering methodologies in exploratory data analysis." Advances in Computers 19: 113-228.

EDELBROCK, C. (1979) "Comparing the accuracy of hierarchical clustering algorithms: the problem of classifying everybody." Multivariate Behavioral Research 14: 367-384.

————and B. McLAUGHLIN (1979) "Intraclass correlations as metrics for hierarchical cluster analysis: parametric comparisons using the mixture model." Paper presented at the Seventh Annual Meeting, Classification Society.

EVERITT, B. (1980) Cluster Analysis. New York: Halsted.

————(1979) "Unresolved problems in cluster analysis." Biometrics 35: 169-181.

FILSINGER, E., J. FAULKNER, and R. WARLAND (1979) "Empirical taxonomy of religious individuals: an investigation among college students." Sociological Analysis 40: 136-146.

FINNEY, J. W. and R. H. MOOS (1979) "Treatment and outcome for empirical subtypes of alcoholic patients." Journal of Consulting and Clinical Psychology 47: 25-38.

FLEISS, J., W. LAWLOR, S. PLATMAN, and R. FIEVE (1971) "On the use of inverted factor analysis for generating typologies. "Journal of Abnormal Psychology 77: 127-132.

FRIEDMAN, H. P. and J. RUBIN (1967) "On some invariant criteria for grouping data." Journal of the American Statistical Association 62: 1159-1178.

GOLDSTEIN, S. G. and J. D. LINDEN (1969) "Multivariate classification of alcoholics by means of the MMPI." Journal of Abnormal Psychology 74: 661-669.

GOODALL, D. (1967) "The distribution of the matching coefficient." Biometrics 23: 647-656.

GOWER, J. C. (1971) "A general coefficient of similarity and some of its properties." Biometrics 27: 857-872.

————(1967) "A comparison of some methods of cluster analysis." Biometrics 23: 623-637.

GUERTIN, W. (1966) "The search for recurring patterns among individual profiles." Educational and Psychological Measurement 26: 151-165.

HALL, D. J. and D. KHANNA (1977) "The ISODATA method of computation for the relative perception of similarities and differences in complex and real data," in K. Enslein, A. Ralston, and H. W. Wilf (eds.) Statistical Methods for Digital Computers, vol. 3. New York: John Wiley.

HAMER, R. and J. CUNNINGHAM (1981) "Cluster analyzing profile data confounded with interrater differences: a comparison of profile association measures." Applied Psychological Measurement 5: 63-72.

HARTIGAN, J. (1975) Clustering Algorithms. New York: John Wiley.

————(1967) "Representation of similarity matrices by trees." Journal of Statistical Computing and Computer Simulation 4: 187-213.

HOLGERSON, M. (1978) "The limited value of cophenetic correlation as a clustering criterion." Pattern Recognition 10: 287-295.

IMSL (1980) IMSL Reference Manual Library 1, Ed. 6. vol. 1 and 2. Houston, TX: Author.

JARDINE, N. and R. SIBSON (1971) Mathematical Taxonomy. New York: John Wiley.

————(1968) "The construction of hierarchic and non-hierarchic classifications." Computer Journal 11: 117-184.

JOHNSON, S. (1967) "Hierarchical clustering schemes." Psychometrika 38: 241-254.

KUIPER, F. and L. FISHER (1975) "A Monte Carlo comparison of six clustering procedures." Biometrics 31: 777-783.

LANCE, G. and W. WILLIAMS (1967) "A general theory of classificatory sorting strategies."Computer Journal 9: 373-380.

LEE, K. (1979) "Multivariate tests for clusters." Journal of the American Statistical Association 74: 708-714.

LING, R. (1975) "An exact probability distribution of the connectivity of random graphs." Journal of Mathematical Psychology 12: 90-98.

LORR, M. (1983) Cluster Analysis for Social Sciences. San Francisco: Jossey-Bass.

————(1966) Explorations in Typing Psychotics. New York: Pergamon.

————and B. RADHAKRISHNAN (1967) "A comparison of two methods of cluster analysis." Educational and Psychological Measurement 27: 47-53.

MAHALANOBIS, P. (1936) "On the generalized distance in statistics." Proceedings of the National Institute of Science, Calcutta 12: 49-55.

MATTHEWS, A. (1979) "Standardization of measures prior to clustering." Biometrics 35: 892.

MEZZICH, J. and H. SOLOMON (1980) Taxonomy and Behavioral Science: Comparative Performance of Grouping Methods. New York: Academic Press.

MILLER, G. A. (1969) "A psychological method to investigate verbal concepts." Journal of Mathematical Psychology 6: 169-191.

MILLIGAN, G. W. (1981) "A Monte Carlo study of thirty internal criterion measures for cluster analysis." Psychometrika 46: 187-199.

————(1980) "An examination of the effect of six types of error perturbation of fifteen clustering algorithms." Psychometrika 45: 325-342.

————and P. O. ISSAC (1980) "The validation of four ultrametric clustering algorithms." Pattern Recognition 12: 41-50.

MOJENA, R. (1977) "Hierarchical grouping methods and stopping rules—an evaluation." Computer Journal 20: 359-363.

————and D. WISHART (1980) "Stopping rules for Ward's clustering method." pp. 426-432 in Proceedings of COMPSTAT 1980. Würzburg, West Germany: Physika-Verlag.

OVERALL, J. and C. KLETT (1972) Applied Multivariate Analysis. New York: McGraw-Hill.

PEEBLES, C. (1972) "Monothetic-divisive analysis of Moundville burials." Newsletter of Computer Archaeology 7: 1-11.

ROGERS, G. and J. D. LINDEN (1973) "Use of multiple discriminant function analysis in the evaluation of three multivariate grouping techniques." Education and Psychological Measurement 33: 787-802.

ROHLF, F. J. (1977) "Computational efficiency of agglomerative clustering algorithms." Technical Report RC-6831. IBM Watson Research Center.

————(1974) "Methods of comparing classifications." Annual Review of Ecology and Systematics 5: 101-113.

————(1970) "Adaptive hierarchical clustering schemes." Systematic Zoology 19: 58-82.

————J. KISHPAUGH, and D. KIRK (1974) "NT-SYS users manual." State University of New York at Stony Brook.

SAS Institute (1982) SAS User's Guide: Statistics. New York: Author.

SCOTT, A. J. and M. J. SYMONS (1971) "Clustering methods based on the likelihood ratio criteria. Biometrics 27: 387-397.

87

SKINNER, H. (1979) "Dimensions and clusters: a hybrid approach to classification." Applied Psychological Measurement 3: 327-341.

——(1978) "Differentiating the contribution of elevation, scatter, and shape in profile similarity." Educational and Psychological Measurement 38: 297-308.

——and R. BLASHFIELD (1982) "Increasing the impact of cluster analysis research: the case of psychiatric classification." Journal of Consulting and Clinical Psychology 50: 727-734.

SNEATH, P. (1957) "The application of computers to taxonomy." Journal of General Microbiology 17: 201-226.

——and R. SOKAL. (1973) Numerical Taxonomy. San Francisco: W. H. Freeman.

SOKAL, R. and C. D. MICHENER (1958) "A statistical method for evaluating systematic relationships." University of Kansas Scientific Bulletin 38: 1409-1438.

SOKAL, R. and F. ROHLF (1962) "The comparison of dendrograms by objective methods." Taxon 11: 33-40.

SOKAL, R. and P. SNEATH (1963) Principles of Numerical Taxonomy. San Francisco: W. H. Freeman.

SPSS, Inc. (1984) SPSSX. New York: McGraw-Hill.

TRYON, R. (1939) Cluster Analysis. New York: McGraw-Hill.

——and D. E. BAILEY (1970) Cluster Analysis. New York: McGraw-Hill.

TVERSKY, A. (1977) "Features of similarity." Psychological Review 84: 327-352.

VELDMAN, D. J. (1967) "FORTRAN programming for the behavioral sciences." New York: Holt, Rinehart and Winston.

WARD, J. (1963) "Hierarchical grouping to optimize an objective function." Journal of the American Statistical Association 58: 236-244.

WHALLON, R. (1972) "A new approach to pottery typology." American Antiquity 37: 13-34.

——(1971) "A computer program for monothetic subdivisive classification in archaeology." Technical Report 1, University of Michigan Museum of Anthropology, Ann Arbor.

WILLIAMS W. (1971) "Principles of clustering." Annual Review of Ecology and Systematics 2: 303-326.

——G. N. LANCE, M. B. DALE, and H. T. CLIFFORD (1971) "Controversy concerning the criteria for taxometric strategies." Computer Journal 14: 162-165.

WISHART, D. (1982) "Supplement, CLUSTAN user manual, Third Edition." Program Library Unit, Edinburgh University.

——(1969) "Mode analysis: a generalization of nearest neighbor which reduces chaining effects," pp. 282-311 in A. Cole (ed.) Numerical Taxonomy. London: Academic Press.

WOLFE, J. H. (1971) "A Monte Carlo study of the sampling distribution of the likelihood ratio for mixtures of multinormal distributions." Naval Personnel and Training Research Laboratory Technical Bulletin STB 72-2. San Diego, California.

——(1970) "Pattern clustering by multivariate mixture analysis." Multivariate Behavioral Research 5: 329-350.

MARK S. ALDENDERFER is Assistant Professor of Anthropology at Northwestern University. His principal research interests are in the application of quantitative and statistical methods to a wide range of archaeological problems, and he has conducted archaeological field research in Ethiopia, Guatemala, Peru, and the United States. He has been published in American Antiquity, World Archaeology, *and* Multivariate Behavioral Research *and in several edited publications on both archaeological and statistical topics.*

ROGER K. BLASHFIELD is Professor of Clinical Psychology in the Department of Psychiatry at the University of Florida. Among his principal research interests are psychiatric classification, cluster analysis, and clinical assessment. He has recently published a book entitled The Classification of Psychopathology *and has published in such journals as* Psychometrika, Journal of Abnormal Psychology, *and* Applied Psychological Measurement.

SAGE JOURNALS

The International Professional Publishers
2111 West Hillcrest Drive, Newbury Park, California 91320

SAGE
25
YEARS OF
INTERNATIONAL
PROFESSIONAL
PUBLISHING

ders from the U.K., Europe, **Sage Publications, Ltd.**
the Middle East, and Africa **28 Banner Street**
should be sent to: **London EC1Y 8QE**
ENGLAND

Orders from India and **Sage Publications**
South Asia should be sent to: **India Private Limited**
P.O. Box 4215
New Delhi 110 048 INDIA

These journals are available from Sage Periodicals Press.
See following pages for journals available from Sage, London.

TRACTS IN SOCIAL GERONTOLOGY
ent Literature on Aging
ished in Cooperation with
National Council on the Aging, Inc.
rovides abstracts and bibliographies of major articles, books,
rts, and other materials on all aspects of gerontology: in-
ng demography, economics, family relations, government
y, health, institutional care, physiology, psychiatric dysfunc-
, psychology, societal attitudes, work and retirement.
terly: March, June, Sept., Dec. *FIRST ISSUE: MARCH 1990*
y rates: Inst. $98 / Ind. $48 ISSN: 1047-4862

INISTRATION & SOCIETY
r: **Gary L. Wamsley,**
inia Polytechnic Institute and State Univ.
eals with administration, bureaucracy, public organization,
public policy — and the impact these have on politics and
ty.
terly: May, Aug., Nov., Feb.
y rates: Inst. $99 / Ind. $39 / ISSN: 0095-3997

LIA: Journal of Women and Social Work
r: **Betty Sancier,** *Univ. of Wisconsin-Milwaukee*
s a publication for and about women social workers and their
ts. Its intent is to bring insight and knowledge to the field
cial work from a feminist perspective and to provide the
arch and tools necessary to make significant changes and
ovements in the delivery of social services.
terly: Feb., May, Aug., Nov.
y Rates: Inst. $64 / Ind. $30 / ISSN: 0886-1099

RICAN BEHAVIORAL SCIENTIST
ocuses, in theme-organized issues prepared under guest
rs, on emerging cross-disciplinary interests, research, and
ems in the social sciences.
nthly: Sept., Nov., Jan., Mar., May, July
y rates: Inst. $108 / Ind. $36 / ISSN: 0002-7642

RICAN POLITICS QUARTERLY
r: **Susan Welch,** *Univ. of Nebraska*
romotes basic research in all areas of American political
vior — including urban, state, and national policies, as well
ressing social problems requiring political solutions.
terly: Jan., April, July, Oct.
y rates: Inst. $98 / Ind. $34 / ISSN: 0044-7803

ANNALS
e **American Academy of Political and Social Science**
r: **Richard D. Lambert**
ociate Editor: **Alan W. Heston**
since 1891, The Annals has served as the preeminent forum
e interdisciplinary discussion of single problems and policy
es affecting America and the world community.
nthly: Jan., March, May, July, Sept., Nov.
y rates: Inst. $72 (p) / $89 (c) Ind. $32 (p) / $45 (c)
: 0002-7162

AVIOR MODIFICATION
rs: **Michel Hersen,** *Western Psychiatric Inst. & Clinic*
S. Bellack, *Medical College of Pennsylvania at EPPI*
escribes (in detail for replication purposes) assessment and
ification techniques for problems in psychiatric, clinical,
ational, and rehabilitational settings.
terly: Jan., April, July, Oct.
y rates: Inst. $100 / Ind. $38 / ISSN: 0145-4455

NA REPORT: A Journal of East Asian Studies
r: **C.R.M. Rao,**
tre for the Study of Developing Societies, Delhi
ncourages the increased understanding of contemporary
a and its East Asian neighbors, their cultures and ways of
lopment, and their impact on India and other South Asian
tries.
terly: Feb., May, Aug., Nov.
y rates: Inst. $59 / Ind. $30 / ISSN: 0009-4455

COMMUNICATION ABSTRACTS
Editor: **Thomas F. Gordon,** *Temple Univ.*
. . .provides coverage of recent literature in all areas of communication studies (both mass and interpersonal). Includes expanded coverage of new communications technologies.
Bimonthly: Feb., April, June, Aug., Oct., Dec.
Yearly rates: Inst. $270 / Ind. $90 / ISSN: 0162-2811

COMMUNICATION RESEARCH
Editor: **Peter R. Monge,** *Annenberg School, USC*
. . .provides an interdisciplinary forum for scholars and professionals to present new research in communication. Encourages
rigorous studies of mass (and interpersonal) communication.
Bimonthly: Feb., April, June, Aug., Oct., Dec.
Yearly rates: Inst. $132 / Ind. $42 / ISSN: 0093-6502

COMPARATIVE POLITICAL STUDIES
Editor: **James A. Caporaso,** *Univ. of Washington*
. . .publishes theoretical and empirical research articles by
scholars engaged in cross-national study, and includes research
notes and review essays.
Quarterly: April, July, Oct, Jan.
Yearly rates: Inst. $96 / Ind. $32 / ISSN: 0010-4140

CONTRIBUTIONS TO INDIAN SOCIOLOGY
Editor: **T. N. Madan,** *Institute of Economic Growth, Delhi*
. . .a distinguished international forum for research on Indian and
South Asian societies.
Biannually: May and November
Yearly rates: Inst. $59 / Ind. $27 / ISSN: 0069-9667

The COUNSELING PSYCHOLOGIST
Journal of Counseling Psychology
of the American Psychological Association (Div. 17)
Editor: **Bruce R. Fretz,** *Univ. of Maryland, College Park*
Editor-elect: **Gerald Stone,** *Univ. of Iowa*
. . .presents timely coverage — especially in new or developing
areas of practice and research — of topics of immediate interest
to counseling psychologists. Defines the field and communicates
that identity to the profession as well as to those in other
disciplines.
Quarterly: Jan., April, July, Oct.
Yearly rates: Inst. $90 / Ind. $32 / ISSN: 0011-0000

CRIME & DELINQUENCY
Published in cooperation with the
National Council on Crime and Delinquency
Editor: **Don C. Gibbons,** *Portland State Univ.*
. . .addresses specific policy or program implications or issues
— social, political, and economic — of great topical interest to
the professional with direct involvement in criminal justice.
Quarterly: Jan., April, July, Oct.
Yearly rates: Inst. $96 / Ind. $36 / ISSN: 0011-1287

CRIMINAL JUSTICE AND BEHAVIOR
Official Publication of the AACP
Published in affiliation with the ACA
Editor: **Allen K. Hess,** *Auburn Univ.*
. . .provides a means of communication among mental health
professionals, behavioral scientists, researchers, and practitioners
in the area of criminal justice.
Quarterly: March, June, Sept., Dec.
Yearly rates: Inst. $95 / Ind. $36 / ISSN: 0093-8548

Sage Periodicals Press A Division of SAGE Publications, Inc.
Newbury Park • London • New Delhi

ECONOMIC DEVELOPMENT QUARTERLY
The Journal of American Economic Revitalization
Editors: Richard D. Bingham, Cleveland State
Sammis B. White, Univ. of Wisconsin-Milwaukee
& Gail Garfield Schwartz, NY State Public Serv. Commission
. . . disseminates information on the latest research, programs, policies, and trends in the field of economic development. EDQ is unique in its concern for all areas of development — large cities, small towns, rural areas, and overseas trade and expansion.
Quarterly: Feb., May, Aug., Nov.
Yearly rates: Inst. $90 / Ind. $36 / ISSN: 0891-2424

EDUCATION and URBAN SOCIETY
. . . provides, through theme-organized issues prepared under guest editors, a forum for social scientific research on education as a social institution within urban environments, the politics of education, and educational institutions and processes as agents of social change.
Quarterly: Nov., Feb., May, Aug.
Yearly rates: Inst. $90 / Ind. $34 / ISSN: 0013-1245

EDUCATIONAL ADMINISTRATION ABSTRACTS
. . . provides abstracts drawn from more than 140 professional Journals relating to educational administration.
Quarterly: Jan., April, July, Oct.
Yearly rates: Inst. $188 / Ind. $66 / ISSN: 0013-1601

EDUCATIONAL ADMINISTRATION QUARTERLY
Published in cooperation with the
University Council for Educational Administration
Editor: Steven T. Bossert, Univ. of Utah
. . . seeks to stimulate critical thought and to disseminate the latest knowledge about research and practice in educational administration.
Quarterly: Feb., May, Aug., Nov.
Yearly rates: Inst. $90 / Ind. $36 / ISSN: 0013-161X

ENVIRONMENT AND BEHAVIOR
Published in cooperation with the
Environmental Design Research Association (edra)
Editor: Robert B. Bechtel, Univ. of Arizona
. . . reports rigorous experimental and theoretical work on the study, design, and control of the physical environment and its interaction with human behavioral systems.
Bimonthly: Jan., Mar., May, July, Sept., Nov.
Yearly rates: Inst. $120 / Ind. $48 / ISSN: 0013-9165

EVALUATION & THE HEALTH PROFESSIONS
Editor: R. Barker Bausell, Univ. of Maryland
. . . provides a forum for all health professionals interested or engaged in the development, implementation, and evaluation of health programs.
Quarterly: March, June, Sept., Dec.
Yearly rates: Inst. $96 / Ind. $36 / ISSN: 0163-2787

EVALUATION REVIEW
A Journal of Applied Social Research
Editors: Richard A. Berk & Howard E. Freeman,
both at Univ. of California, Los Angeles
. . . a forum for researchers, planners, and policymakers engaged in the development, implementation, and utilization of evaluation studies. Reflects a wide range of methodological and conceptual approaches to evaluation and its many applications.
Bimonthly: Feb., April, June, Aug., Oct., Dec.
Yearly rates: Inst. $120 / Ind. $45 / ISSN: 0193-841X

GENDER & SOCIETY
Official Publication of Sociologists for Women in Society
Editor: Judith Lorber,
Graduate School and Brooklyn College, CUNY
. . . focuses on the social and structural study of gender as a basic principle of the social order and as a primary social category. Emphasizing theory and research, G&S aims to advance both the study of gender and feminist scholarship.
Quarterly: March, June, Sept., Dec.
Yearly rates: Inst. $84 / Ind. $32 / ISSN: 0891-2432

GROUP & ORGANIZATION STUDIES
An International Journal
Editor: Michael J. Kavanagh, SUNY, Albany
. . . bridges the gap between research and practice for psychologists, group facilitators, educators, and consultants who are involved in the broad field of human relations training.
Quarterly: March, June, Sept., Dec.
Yearly rates: Inst. $100 / Ind. $42 / ISSN: 0364-1082

HISPANIC JOURNAL OF BEHAVIORAL SCIENCES
Editor: Amado M. Padilla, Stanford University
. . . publishes research articles, case histories, critical reviews scholarly notes that are of theoretical interest or deal methodological issues related to Hispanic populations.
Quarterly: Feb., May, Aug., Nov.
Yearly rates: Inst. $60 / Ind. $30 / ISSN: 0739-9863

HUMAN COMMUNICATION RESEARCH
Editor: James Bradac, Univ. of Calif, Santa Barbara
. . . publishes important research and high-quality reports contribute to the expanding body of knowledge about hur communication.
Quarterly: Sept., Dec., March, June
Yearly rates: Inst. $96 / Ind. $36 / ISSN: 0360-3989

HUMAN RESOURCES ABSTRACTS
. . . contains abstracts of the most important recent literature the professional who needs easy reference to current and cha ing ideas in the diverse area of manpower and human resour development, and related social/governmental policy questic
Quarterly: March, June, Sept., Dec.
Yearly rates: Inst. $188 / Ind. $66 / ISSN: 0099-2453

INDIAN ECONOMIC AND SOCIAL HISTORY REVIEW
Editor: Dharma M. Kumar, Delhi School of Economics
. . . focuses on the history, economy, and society of India South Asia, and includes comparative studies of wc development.
Quarterly: March, June, Sept., Dec.
Yearly rates: Inst. $70 / Ind. $35 / ISSN: 0019-4646

THE INDIAN JOURNAL OF SOCIAL SCIENCE
Sponsored by the Indian Council of Social Science Resea
Editor: Sukhamoy Chakravarty, Univ. of Delhi
. . . promotes scientific discussion on the diverse concerns social science research — the problems of development social change, the interface between science, society, culture technology, and a comprehension of future patterns of devel ment as they relate to the developing countries.
Quarterly: March, June, Sept., Dec.
Yearly Rates: Inst. $59 / Ind. $35

INTERNATIONAL STUDIES
Editor: Anirudha Gupta, School of International Studies, Jawaharlal Nehru Univ., New Delhi
. . . the most outstanding Indian research journal in the field international affairs and area studies.
Quarterly: Jan., April, July, Oct.
Yearly rates: Inst. $70 / Ind. $35 / ISSN: 0020-8817

JOURNAL OF ADOLESCENT RESEARCH
Editor: E. Ellen Thornburg, Tucson, Arizona
. . . provides professionals with the most current and relevant formation on ways in which individuals ages 10-20 devel behave, and are influenced by societal and cultural perspectiv
Quarterly: Jan., April, July, Oct.
Yearly Rates: Inst. $78 / Ind. $36 / ISSN: 0743-5584

JOURNAL OF AGING AND HEALTH
Editor: Kyriakos S. Markides,
Univ. of Texas Medical Branch, Galveston
. . . deals with social and behavioral factors related to aging a health, emphasizing health and quality of life.
Quarterly: Feb., May, Aug., Nov.
Yearly Rates: Inst. $78 / Ind. $36 / ISSN: 0898-2643

JOURNAL OF APPLIED GERONTOLOGY
The Official Journal of the Southern Gerontological Soci
Editor: Miles Simpson, North Carolina Central Univ.
. . . strives to consistently publish articles in all subdisciplines aging whose findings, conclusions, or suggestions have clear sometimes immediate applicability to the problems encounte by older persons.
Quarterly: March, June, Sept., Dec.
Yearly rates: Inst. $88 / Ind. $38 / ISSN: 0733-4648

JOURNAL OF BLACK STUDIES
Editor: Molefi Kete Asante, Temple Univ.
. . . sustains full analytical discussion of economic, politic sociological, historical, literary, and philosophical issues rela to persons of African descent.
Quarterly: Sept., Dec., March, June
Yearly rates: Inst. $92 / Ind. $34 / ISSN: 0021-9347

JOURNAL OF CONFLICT RESOLUTION
Journal of The Peace Science Society (International)
Editor: Bruce M. Russett, Yale University
. . . draws from interdisciplinary sources in its focus on the analy of causes, prevention, and solution of international, domestic, a interpersonal conflicts.
Quarterly: March, June, Sept., Dec.
Yearly rates: Inst. $116 / Ind. $40 / ISSN: 0022-0027

URNAL OF CONTEMPORARY ETHNOGRAPHY
(**rmerly Urban Life**)
tors: Patricia Adler, Univ of Colorado, Boulder
Peter Adler, Univ. of Denver
the first journal dedicated to ethnography and qualitative
earch in general. Advances sociological knowledge through
ensive, in-depth studies of human behavior in natural settings.
arterly: April, July, Oct., Jan.
rly rates: Inst. $105 / Ind. $34 / ISSN: 0891-2416

URNAL OF CROSS-CULTURAL PSYCHOLOGY
blished for the Center for Cross-Cultural Research,
estern Washington University
itor: **Juris G. Draguns,** Pennsylvania State Univ.
nior Editor: **Walter J. Lonner,** Western Washington U.
.presents behavioral and social research concentrating on
/chological phenomena as differentially conditioned by culture,
d on the individual as a member of the cultural group.
arterly: March, June, Sept., Dec.
arly rates: Inst. $94 / Ind. $35 / ISSN: 0022-0221

URNAL OF EARLY ADOLESCENCE
litor: **E. Ellen Thornburg,** Tucson, Arizona
.provides a well-balanced, interdisciplinary, international
rspective on early adolescent development (age 10 through 14
ars) and the factors affecting it.
arterly: Feb., May, Aug., Nov.
arly rates: Inst. $68 / Ind. $32 / ISSN: 0272-4316

URNAL OF FAMILY ISSUES
onsored by the National Council on Family Relations
litor: **Patricia A. Voydanoff,** Univ. of Dayton
.devoted to contemporary social issues and social problems
ated to marriage and family life, and to theoretical and profes-
onal issues of current interest to those who work with and study
milies.
arterly: March, June, Sept., Dec.
arly rates: Inst. $95 / Ind. $35 / ISSN: 0192-513X

JURNAL OF FAMILY PSYCHOLOGY
ournal of the Division of Family Psychology of the
merican Psychological Association (Div. 43)
litor: **Howard A. Liddle,** Temple Univ.
.enhances theory, research, and clinical practice in family
ychology and deals with: family and marital theory and con-
pts; research and evaluation; therapeutic frame works and
ethods; training and supervision; policies and legal matters con-
rning the family and marriage.
arterly: Sept., Dec., March, June
arly rates: Inst. $80 / Ind. $36 / ISSN: 0893-3200

JURNAL OF HUMANISTIC PSYCHOLOGY
blished in cooperation with the
sociation for Humanistic Psychology
litor: **Thomas Greening,** Psychological Service Associates
.provides an interdisciplinary forum for contributions and con-
versies in humanistic psychology as applied to personal growth,
erpersonal encounter, social problems, and philosophical
sues.
arterly: Jan, April, July, Oct.
arly rates: Inst. $90 / Ind. $34 / ISSN: 0022-1678

JURNAL OF INTERPERSONAL VIOLENCE
oncerned with the Study and Treatment of Victims and
erpetrators of Physical and Sexual Violence
litor: **Jon R. Conte,** Univ. of Chicago
.provides a forum for discussion of the concerns and activities
professionals and researchers working in domestic violence,
ild sexual abuse, rape and sexual assault, physical child abuse,
d violent crime.
arterly: March, June, Sept., Dec.
arly rates: Inst. $80 / Ind. $35 / ISSN: 0886-2605

JURNAL OF MENTAL HEALTH COUNSELING
fficial Publication of the
merican Mental Health Counselors Association
litor: **Lawrence Gerstein,** Ball State University
.disseminates pertinent theory, therapeutic applications, and
search related to mental health counseling.
arterly: Jan., Apr., July, Oct.
arly rates: Inst. $60 / Ind. $26 / ISSN: 0193-1830

JOURNAL OF URBAN HISTORY
Editor: Blaine A. Brownell, Univ. of Alabama, Birmingham
. . .studies the history of cities and urban societies in all periods
of human history and in all geographical areas of the world.
Quarterly: Nov., Feb., May, Aug.
Yearly rates: Inst. $98 / Ind. $34 / ISSN: 0096-1442

JOURNAL OF RESEARCH IN CRIME AND DELINQUENCY
Published in Cooperation with the
National Council on Crime and Delinquency
Editor: Vincent O'Leary, SUNY Albany
. . .reports on original research in crime and delinquency, new
theory, and the critical analyses of theories and concepts especial-
ly pertinent to research development in this field.
Quarterly: Feb., May, Aug., Nov.
Yearly rates: Inst. $95 / Ind $36 / ISSN: 0022-4278

KNOWLEDGE:
Creation, Diffusion, Utilization
Editor: Robert Rich, Univ. of Illinois
. . .provides a forum for researchers, policymakers, R&D
managers, and practitioners engaged in the process of knowledge
development which includes the processes of creation, diffusion,
and utilization.
Quarterly: Sept., Dec., March, June
Yearly rates: Inst. $95 / Ind. $38 / ISSN: 0164-0259

LATIN AMERICAN PERSPECTIVES
A Journal on Capitalism and Socialism
Managing Editor: Ronald H. Chilcote,
Univ. of California, Riverside
. . .discusses and debates critical issues relating to capitalism,
imperialism, and socialism as they affect individuals, societies,
and nations throughout the Americas.
Quarterly: Jan., April, July, Oct.
Yearly rates: Inst. $95 / Ind. $32 / ISSN: 0094-582X

MANAGEMENT COMMUNICATION QUARTERLY
An International Journal
Editors: Paul C. Feingold, USC
Christine Kelly, New York Univ.
Larry R. Smeltzer, Arizona State Univ.
JoAnne Yates, MIT
. . .brings together communication research from a wide variety
of fields, with a focus on managerial and organizational effec-
tiveness. Includes book reviews and notes from professionals in
the field.
Quarterly: Aug., Nov., Feb., May
Yearly rates: Inst. $85 / Ind. $32 / ISSN: 0893-3189

MODERN CHINA
An International Quarterly of History and Social Science
Editor: Philip C. C. Huang, Univ. of California, Los Angeles
. . .encourages a new interdisciplinary scholarship and dialogue
on China's ongoing revolutionary experience.
Quarterly: Jan., April, July, Oct.
Yearly rates: Inst. $98 / Ind. $39 / ISSN: 0097-7004

PEACE & CHANGE
Sponsored by the Council on Peace Research in History
(CPRH) & the Consortium on Peace Research, Education and
Development (COPRED)
Editors: Robert D. Schulzinger & Paul Wehr,
University of Colorado-Boulder
. . .publishes scholarly and interpretive articles related to the
achieving of a peaceful, just, and humane society. It seeks to
transcend national, disciplinary, and occupational boundaries and
to build bridges between peace research, education, and action.
Quarterly: Jan., Apr., July, Oct.
Yearly rates: Inst. $60 / Ind. $30 / ISSN: 0149-0508

PERSONALITY AND SOCIAL PSYCHOLOGY BULLETIN
Journal of the Society for Personality and Social Psychology
Editor: Richard E. Petty, Ohio State Univ.
. . .publishes theoretical articles and empirical reports of research
in all areas of personality and social psychology.
Quarterly: March, June, Sept., Dec.
Yearly rates: Inst. $120 / Ind. $44 / ISSN: 0146-1672

PERSON-CENTERED REVIEW
An International Journal of Research, Theory, and Application
Editor: David J. Cain
. . . is devoted to the continued development of person-centered
theory, research, and application in the fields of psychotherapy,
education, supervision and training, and human development in
various group and organizational settings.
Quarterly: Feb., May, Aug., Nov.
Yearly rates: Inst. $80 / Ind. $35 / ISSN: 0883-2293

PHILOSOPHY OF THE SOCIAL SCIENCES   **New**
Editors: John O'Neill, I.C Jarvie,
J.N. Hattiangadi, J.O. Wisdom, York University, Toronto
. . .publishes articles, discussions, symposia, literature surveys,
and more of interest both to philosophers concerned with the
social sciences and to social scientists concerned with the
philosophical foundations of their subject.
Quarterly: March, June, Sept., Dec.
Yearly rates: Inst. $70 / Ind. $35 / ISSN: 0048-3931

POLITICAL THEORY
An International Journal of Political Philosophy
Editor: **Tracy B. Strong**, *Univ. of Calif., San Diego*
. . . provides a forum for the diverse orientations in the study of political ideas, including the history of political thought, modern theory, conceptual analysis, and polemic argumentation.
Quarterly: Feb., May, Aug., Nov.
Yearly rates: Inst. $98 / Ind. $35 / ISSN: 0090-5917

PSYCHOLOGY AND DEVELOPING SOCIETIES
A Journal Published by the Centre of Advanced Study in Psychology, Univ. of Allahabad, India
Chief Editor: **Durganand Sinha**, *National Fellow,*
Indian Council for Social Science Research, New Delhi,
. . . provides a forum for psychologists from different parts of the world who are concerned with problems of developing societies. The journal will publish theoretical, empirical, and review papers which help to further understanding of the problems of these societies.
FIRST ISSUE: March, 1989 / Bi-Annual: March, Sept.
Yearly rates: Inst. $49 / Ind. $24

PUBLIC FINANCE QUARTERLY
Editor: **J. Ronnie Davis**, *Univ. of New Orleans—Lakefront*
. . . studies the theory, policy, and institutions related to the allocation, distribution, and stabilization functions within the public sector of the economy.
Quarterly: Jan., April, July, Oct.
Yearly rates: Inst. $115 / Ind. $44 / ISSN: 0048-5853

RATIONALITY AND SOCIETY
Editor: **James S. Coleman**, *University of Chicago*
. . . focuses on the growing contributions of rational-action based theory, and the questions and controversies surrounding this growth. The journal publishes work in social theory and social research based on the rational-action paradigm, as well as work challenging this paradigm.
First Issue, July 1989
2 issues in 1989: July, Oct. Quarterly in 1990
Rates: Inst. $141 / Ind. $57 (Vol 1&2-6 issues) / ISSN: 1043-4631

RESEARCH ON AGING
A Quarterly of Social Gerontology and Adult Development
Editors: **Rhonda J.V. Montgomery**, *Inst. of Gerontology, Wayne State Univ.*
& Edgar F. Borgatta, *Inst. on Aging, Univ. of Washington,*
. . . a journal of interdisciplinary research on current issues, methodological and research problems in the study of the aged.
Quarterly: March, June, Sept., Dec.
Yearly rates: Inst. $98 / Ind. $35 / ISSN: 0164-0275

SAGE FAMILY STUDIES ABSTRACTS
. . . abstracts major articles, reports, books and other materials on policy, theory, and research relating to the family, traditional and alternative lifestyles, therapy and counseling.
Quarterly: Feb., May, Aug., Nov.
Yearly rates: Inst. $188 / Ind. $66 / ISSN: 0164-0283

SAGE PUBLIC ADMINISTRATION ABSTRACTS
. . . publishes cross-indexed abstracts covering recent literature (plus related citations) on all aspects of public administration. Entries are drawn from books, articles, pamphlets, government publications, significant speeches, legislative research studies, and other fugitive material.
Quarterly: April, July, Oct., Jan.
Yearly rates: Inst. $188 / Ind. $66 / ISSN: 0094-6958

SAGE URBAN STUDIES ABSTRACTS
. . . publishes cross-indexed abstracts of important recent literature (plus related citations) on all aspects of urban studies: government and administration, policy, transportation, spatial analysis, planning, social analysis, community studies, education, finance and economics, law, management, environment, and comparative urban analysis.
Quarterly: Feb., May, Aug., Nov.
Yearly rates: Inst. $188 / Ind. $66 / ISSN: 0090-5747

SCIENCE, TECHNOLOGY, & HUMAN VALUES
Sponsored by the Society for Social Studies of Science (4S)
Editor: **Susan E. Cozzens**, *Rensselaer Polytechnic Institute*
. . . contains research and commentary on the development and dynamics of science and technology, including their involvement in politics, society, and culture.
Quarterly: Jan., Apr., July, Oct.
Yearly rates: Inst. $80 / Ind. $39 / ISSN: 0162-2439

SIMULATION & GAMING
An International Journal of Theory, Design, & Research
Official Journal of ABSEL, NASAGA, and ISAGA.
Editor: **David Crookall**, *Univ. of Alabama*
. . . publishes theoretical and empirical papers related to man, man-machine, and machine simulations of social processes; featured are theoretical papers about simulations in research and teaching, empirical studies, and technical papers on new gaming techniques.
Quarterly: March, June, Sept., Dec.
Yearly rates: Inst. $105 / Ind. $36 / ISSN: 1046-8781

SMALL GROUP RESEARCH
An International Journal of Theory, Investigation, and Application (Incorporating Small Group Behavior and International Journal of Small Group Research)
Editors: **Charles Garvin**, *Univ. of Michigan and*
Richard Brian Polley, *Lewis & Clark College*
. . . presents research, theoretical advancements, and empirically supported applications with respect to all types of small groups. Through advancing the systematic study of small groups, the interdisciplinary journal seeks to increase communication among all who are professionally interested in group phenomena.
Quarterly: Feb., May, Aug. Nov.
Yearly rates: Inst. $98 / Ind. $38 / ISSN: 1046-4964

SMR/SOCIOLOGICAL METHODS AND RESEARCH
Editor: **J. Scott Long**, *Indiana Univ.*
. . . a leading journal of quantitative research and methodology in the social sciences.
Quarterly: Aug., Nov., Feb., May
Yearly rates: Inst. $100 / Ind. $38 / ISSN: 0049-1241

SOUTH ASIA JOURNAL
A Quarterly of the Indian Council for South Asian Cooperation
Editor: **Professor Bimal Prasad**, *School of International Studies, Jawaharlal Nehru Univ.*
. . . provides analyses of regional and national political, economic, historical, and cultural issues among the nations of South Asia.
Quarterly: July, Oct., Jan., April
Yearly rates: Inst. $65 / Ind. $30 / ISSN: 0970-4868

STUDIES IN HISTORY
Editor: **S. Gopal**, *Centre for Historical Studies, Jawaharlal Nehru Univ., New Delhi*
. . . reflects the expansion and diversification that has occurred in historical research in India in recent years.
Biannually: February and August
Yearly rates: Inst. $54 / Ind. $27 / ISSN: 0257-6430

URBAN AFFAIRS QUARTERLY
Editors: **Dennis R. Judd and Donald Phares**, *both at Univ. of Missouri, St. Louis*
. . . emphasizes state-of-the-art research and scholarly analysis on urban themes: urban life, metropolitan systems, urban economic development, and urban policy. Historical and cross-cultural perspectives add to its interdisciplinary features.
Quarterly: Sept., Dec., March, June
Yearly rates: Inst. $96 / Ind. $34 / ISSN: 0042-0816

URBAN EDUCATION
Editor: **Warren Button**, *SUNY Buffalo*
. . . exists to improve the quality of urban education by making the results of relevant empirical and scholarly inquiry from a variety of fields more widely available.
Quarterly: April, July, Oct., Jan.
Yearly rates: Inst. $98 / Ind. 34 / ISSN: 0042-0859

WESTERN JOURNAL OF NURSING RESEARCH
A Forum for Communicating Nursing Research
Editor: **Pamela J. Brink**, *Univ. of Alberta*
. . . an innovative forum for scholarly debate, as well as research and theoretical papers. Clinical studies have commentaries and rebuttals. Departments deal with current issues in nursing research.
Bimonthly: Feb., Apr., June., Aug., Oct., Dec.
Yearly rates: Inst. $108 / Ind. $48 ISSN: 0193-9459

WORK AND OCCUPATIONS
An International Sociological Journal
Editor: **Curt Tausky**, *Univ. of Massachusetts, Amherst*
. . . an international forum for sociological research and theory in the substantive areas of work, occupations, leisure — their structures and interrelationships.
Quarterly. Feb., May., Aug., Nov.
Yearly rates: Inst. $90 / Ind. $34 / ISSN: 0730-8884

WRITTEN COMMUNICATION
A Quarterly Journal of Research, Theory, & Application
Editors: **Roger D. Cherry & Keith Walters**, *Ohio State Univ.* and **Stephen P. Witte**
. . . provides a forum for the free exchange of ideas, theoretical viewpoints, and methodological approaches that better define and further develop thought and practice in the exciting study of written word.
Quarterly: Jan., April., July., Oct.
Yearly rates: Inst. $96 / Ind. $36 / ISSN: 0741-0883

YOUTH & SOCIETY
Editor: **David Gottlieb**, *Univ. of Houston*
. . . brings together interdisciplinary empirical studies and theoretical papers on the broad social and political implications of youth culture and development; concentration is primarily on the age span from mid-adolescence through young adulthood.
Quarterly: Sept., Dec., March., June
Yearly rates: Inst. $96 / Ind. $34 / ISSN: 0044-118X

urnals Available
om Sage, London

LETIN OF PEACE PROPOSALS
ished under the auspices of the
national Peace Research Association
or: **Magne Barth,** *International Peace*
earch Institute, Olso
terly: March, June, Sept., Dec.

RENT SOCIOLOGY
urnal of The International
ological Association
or: **William Outhwaite,**
versity of Sussex
e times a year: Spring, Summer, Winter

ELOPMENT AND CHANGE
ished on behalf of the
tute of Social Studies, The Hague
ors: **Martin Doornbos,**
< Van Roosmalen,
Ashwani Saith
itute of Social Studies
terly: Jan, April, July, Oct.

ELOPMENT POLICY REVIEW
Journal of the
seas Development Institute
or: **Sheila Page,**
rseas Development Institute
terly: March, June, Sept., Dec.

COURSE AND SOCIETY
national Journal for the Study of
ourse and Communication in their
al, Political and Cultural Contexts
or: **Teune A Van Dijk,**
versity of Amsterdam
terly: Jan., April, July, Oct.
issue: July 1990

NOMIC AND INDUSTRIAL
OCRACY
nternational Journal
or: **Rudolf Meidner,**
etslivscentrum (The Swedish Centre
Working Life) Stockholm
terly: Feb., May, Aug., Nov.

OPEAN HISTORY QUARTERLY
or: **R.M. Blinkhorn,**
versity of Lancaster
terly: Jan., April, July, Oct.

OPEAN JOURNAL
COMMUNICATION
ors: **Jay G. Blumler,**
versity of Leeds,
s McQuail,
versity of Amsterdam
Karl Erik Rosengren,
versity of Lund
terly: March, June, Sept., Dec.

UP ANALYSIS
Journal of Group
ytic Psychotherapy
or: **Malcom Pines,** *The Tavistock Clinic*
terly: March, June, Sept., Dec.

ERNATIONAL REVIEW OF
MINISTRATIVE SCIENCES
or: **James Sundquist,**
okings Institution, Washington
terly: March, June, Sept., Dec.

ERNATIONAL SOCIAL WORK
or: **Francis Turner,**
k University, Ontario
terly: Jan., April, July, Oct.

ERNATIONAL SOCIOLOGY
urnal of the International
ological Association
or: **Martin Albrow,**
versity College, Cardiff
terly: March, June, Sept., Dec.

RNAL OF
TEMPORARY HISTORY
ors: **Walter Laqueur and**
rge L. Mosse,
versity of Wisconsin
terly: Jan., April, July, Oct.

(More on reverse)

T9312

JOURNAL ORDER FORM

NAME _____

ADDRESS _____

INSTITUTION _____

CITY _____ STATE _____ ZIP _____

Rates Effective September 1, 1989 — August 31, 1990

Rates subject to change without notice.

Rate: ☐ Institutional ☐ Individual ☐ 1 year ☐ 2 year ☐ 3 year

Personal orders must be paid by personal check, MasterCard, or Visa.

☐ Check enclosed. ☐ Please invoice. ☐ My credit card information is enclosed.
Charge to my ☐ MasterCard ☐ Visa

Acct. No. _____ Exp. Date _____

Signature _____

I would like more information on the following journals:

SAGE
Publications, Inc.

For subscriptions outside the U.S., please add postage of $6 for quarterlies, $9 for bi-
monthlies, per year.

3/90

PLEASE ENTER MY SUBSCRIPTION TO:

☐ Abstr in Soc Gerontology
☐ Administration & Society
☐ AFFILIA
☐ Amer Behavioral Scientist
☐ Amer Politics Quarterly
☐ The Annals-Paper
☐ The Annals-Cloth
☐ Behavior Modification
☐ China Report
☐ Communication Abstr.
☐ Communication Research
☐ Comparative Pol Studies
☐ Contributions to Indian Soc
☐ Counseling Psychologist
☐ Crime & Delinquency
☐ Criminal Justice & Behavior
☐ Economic Dev Qtrly
☐ Educ Admin Abst
☐ Educ Admin Qtrly
☐ Educ & Urban Soc
☐ Environment & Behavior
☐ Eval & Hlth Prof
☐ Evaluation Review
☐ Gender & Society
☐ Group & Org Studies

☐ Hispanic Jrnl of Beh Sci
☐ Human Communication Res
☐ Human Resources Abstr
☐ Indian Econ & Soc Hist Rev
☐ Ind Jrnl Soc Sci
☐ International Studies
☐ Jrnl of Adolescent Res
☐ Jrnl of Aging & Health
☐ Jrnl of Applied Gerontolgy
☐ Jrnl of Black Studies
☐ Jrnl of Conflict Resolution
☐ Jrnl of Contemp Ethnogr
☐ Jrnl of Cross-Cultural Psy
☐ Jrnl of Early Adolescence
☐ Jrnl of Family Issues
☐ Jrnl of Family Psychology
☐ Jrnl of Humanistic Psych
☐ Jrnl of Interpersonal Viol
☐ Jrnl of Mntl Health Counseling
☐ Jrnl of Res in Crime & Del
☐ Journal of Urban History
☐ Knowledge
☐ Latin Amer Perspectives
☐ Management Comm Qtrly
☐ Modern China
☐ Peace & Change

☐ Pers and Soc Psy Bulletin
☐ Person-Centered Review
☐ Philos of Soc Science
☐ Political Theory
☐ Psych & Develop Societies
☐ Public Finance Quarterly
☐ Rationality & Society
☐ Research on Aging
☐ Sage Family Studies Abstr
☐ Sage Public Admin Abstr
☐ Sage Urban Studies Abstr
☐ Science, Tech, & Hum Val
☐ Simulation & Gaming
☐ Small Group Research
☐ SMR: Soc Meth and Res
☐ South Asia Journal
☐ Studies in History
☐ Urban Affairs Quarterly
☐ Urban Education
☐ West Jour of Nursing Res
☐ Work and Occupations
☐ Written Communications
☐ Youth & Society

Quantitative Applications
in the Social Sciences

(a Sage University Papers Series)

$7.50 each

SAGE PUBLICATIONS, INC.
P.O. BOX 5084
NEWBURY PARK, CALIFORNIA 91359—9924

Place
Stamp
here